# FARM TO TABLE KIDS COOKBOOK

Illustrated by Natalie Briscoe

cottage door press®

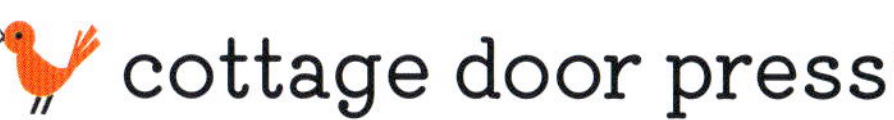

Published 2025 by Cottage Door Press, LLC
5005 Newport Drive, Rolling Meadows, Illinois 60008
www.cottagedoorpress.com



Edited by Alex Messina-Schultheis
Photography by Powell Jordano and Mike Cooper
Additional photography used under license from Shutterstock.com



ISBN 979-8-89019-088-8



## Notes for the Reader

This book uses standard kitchen measuring spoons and cups. All spoon and cup measurements are level unless otherwise indicated. Unless otherwise stated, milk is assumed to be whole, butter is assumed to be unsalted, eggs are large, individual vegetables are medium, and pepper is freshly ground black pepper. Unless otherwise stated, all root vegetables should be peeled prior to using. People with nut allergies should be aware that some of the prepared ingredients used in the recipes in this book may contain nuts. Always check the packaging before use.

For the best results, use a meat thermometer when cooking meat and poultry—check the latest USDA government guidelines for current advice regarding safe minimum internal temperatures. Recipes using raw or very lightly cooked eggs should be avoided by infants, the elderly, pregnant women, and people with weakened immune systems.

Garnishes and serving suggestions are all optional and not necessarily included in the recipe ingredients or method. The times given are only an approximate guide. Preparation times differ according to the techniques used by different people and the cooking times may also vary from those given. Optional ingredients, variations, or serving suggestions have not been included in the time calculations.

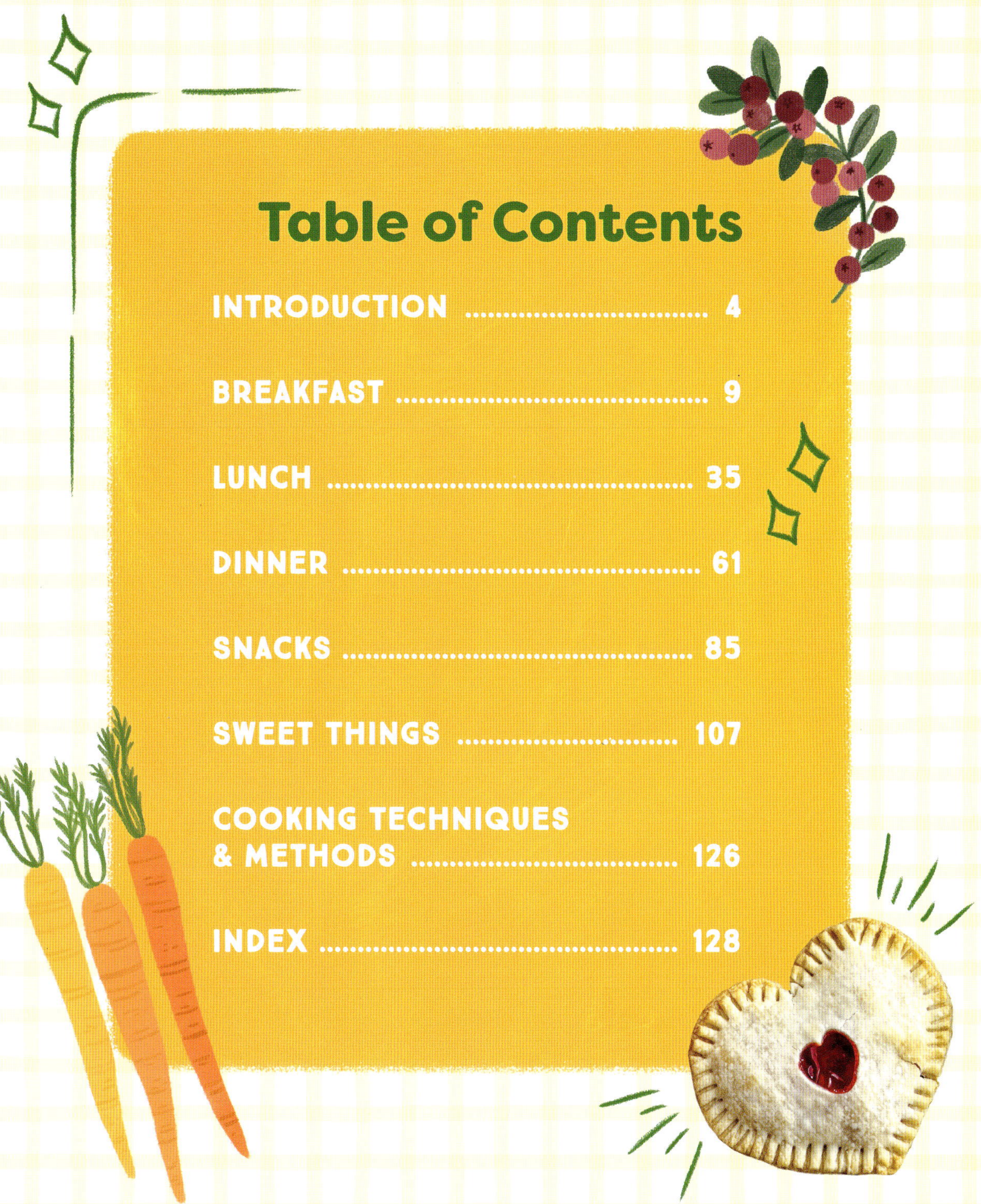

# Table of Contents

# John Deere

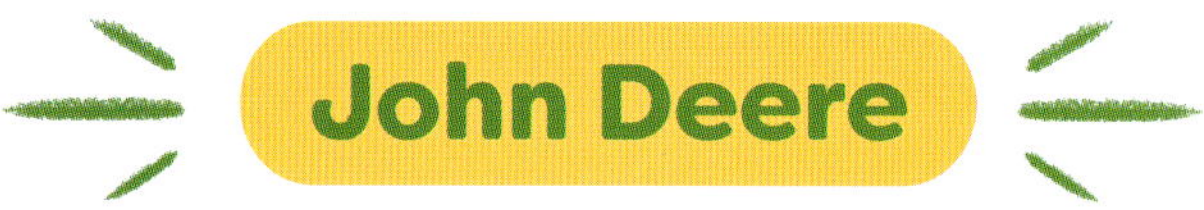

John Deere Kids books encourage kids to get out and do something, stand up and help someone, and use their imagination to change the world. This cookbook aims to improve children's food literacy and help them understand not only what goes into the meals they eat, but how those ingredients start from small seeds before making it to their table. And when kids are involved in making their own food, they will be more excited to eat it!

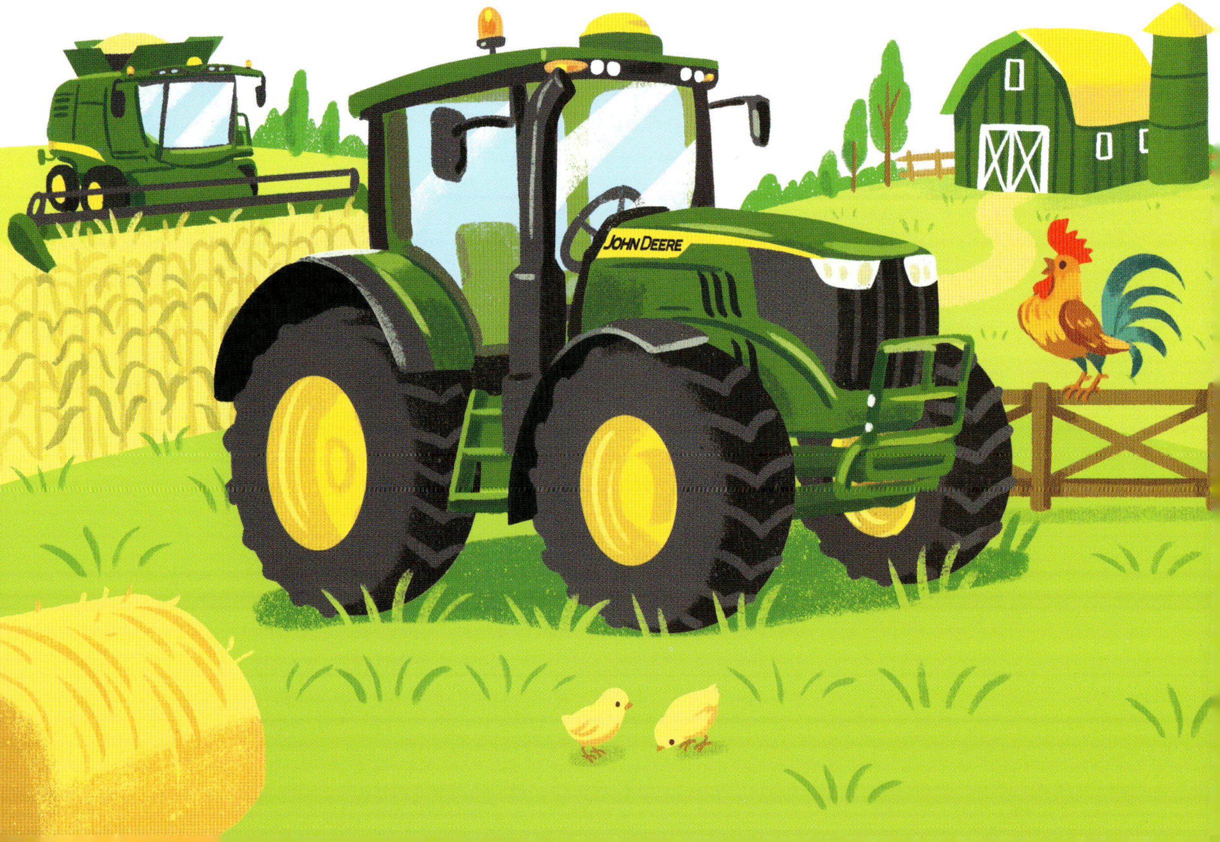

# Using This Book with Kids

This book is for families. Cooking together builds strong relationships and is a great way to pass on traditions. The sooner children get involved in the kitchen, the stronger and healthier their lifelong relationship with food will become.

Some of the recipes in this book are highlighted with one (or more) of the icons below. The adult helper should decide when kids are ready for these steps and when an adult needs to take the lead. Chopped or sliced ingredients in the list should be prepped by an adult or with supervision.

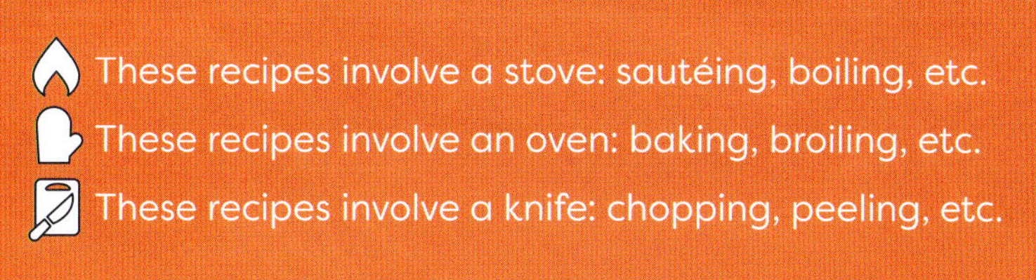

These recipes involve a stove: sautéing, boiling, etc.

These recipes involve an oven: baking, broiling, etc.

These recipes involve a knife: chopping, peeling, etc.

Most importantly, remember to have fun! Even if your dishes don't turn out exactly as expected, your memories of cooking together will be what you treasure forever.

# In the Garden

Based on where fruits and vegetables are growing, there are specific times of year when it's best to plant and harvest them. Let's look at the best seasons to grow and pick some favorite fruits and vegetables!

When a fruit or vegetable is the freshest, it's called "in season."

Each recipe in this book has an icon that shows which time of year its ingredients are most in season.

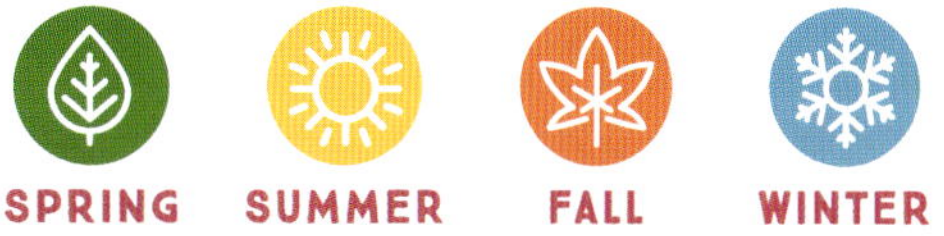

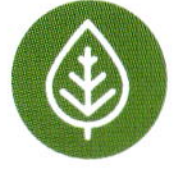

SPRING
SUMMER
FALL
WINTER

## Harvest Time

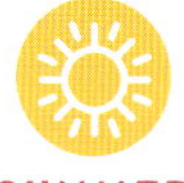

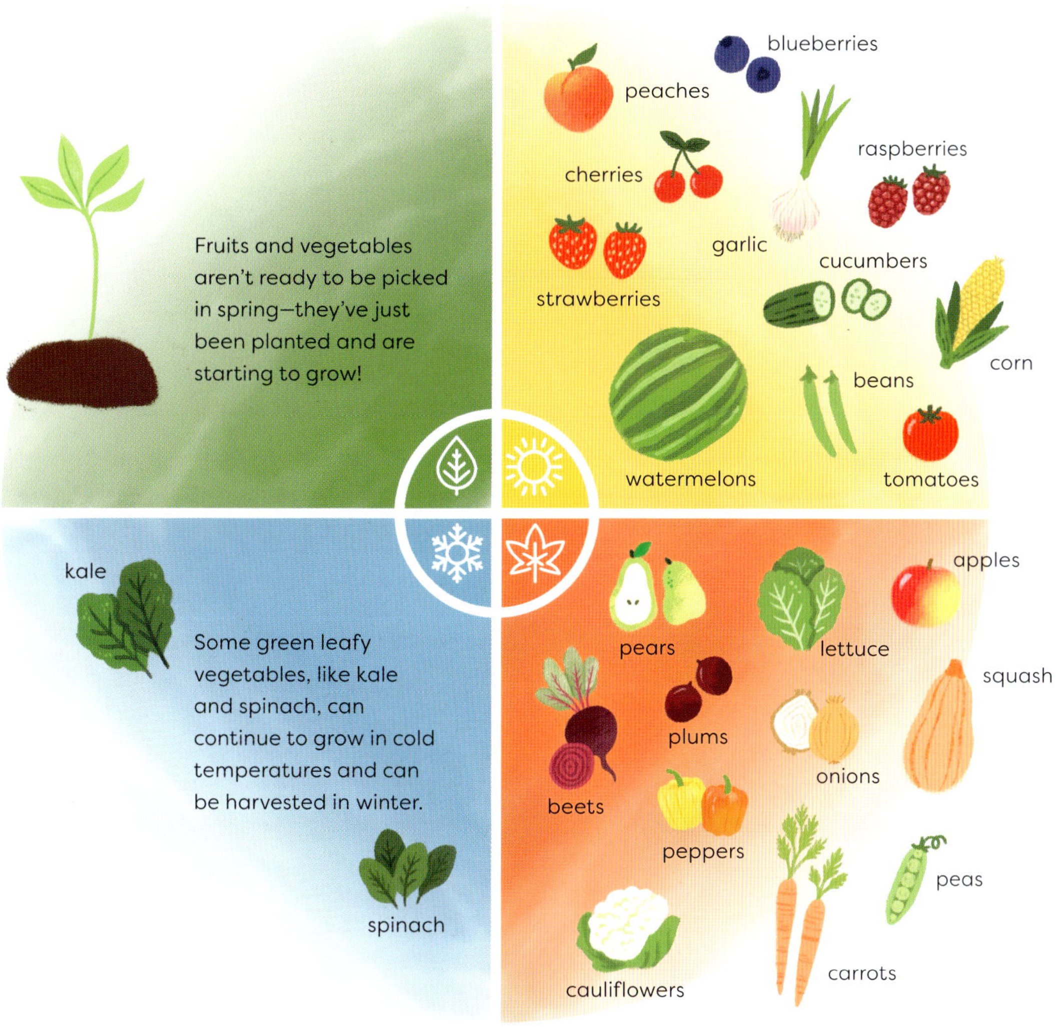
Fruits and vegetables aren't ready to be picked in spring—they've just been planted and are starting to grow!
blueberries
peaches
raspberries
cherries
garlic
strawberries
cucumbers
corn
beans
watermelons
tomatoes
kale
Some green leafy vegetables, like kale and spinach, can continue to grow in cold temperatures and can be harvested in winter.
spinach
apples
pears
lettuce
squash
plums
onions
beets
peppers
peas
carrots
cauliflowers

# What Do Farmers Do All Year?

There is always something to do on the farm! Farmers stay very busy throughout the year. Here are some things they do:

PLANT SEEDS

REPAIR FARM MACHINERY

SPREAD FERTILIZER

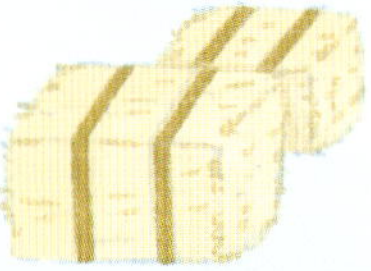

MOW FIELDS

HARVEST CROPS

DELIVER HARVESTED CROPS TO MARKETS

GET THE GROUND READY FOR PLANTING

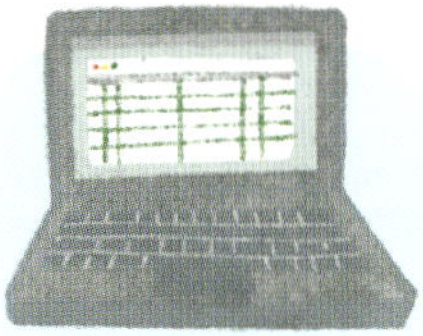

PLAN THEIR CROPS FOR THE YEAR

CUT WEEDS

BREAKFAST
FLOUR
SUGAR

# Pea & Spinach Mini Frittatas

**Makes:** 12 frittatas
**Prep:** 10 mins
**Bake:** 25–30 mins

**Ingredients**
butter, for greasing
1 tablespoon olive oil
4 green onions, trimmed and chopped
½ cup frozen **peas**, thawed
¼ cup spinach, shredded
6 eggs
½ cup milk
½ cup feta cheese, crumbled
salt and pepper, to taste

1. Preheat the oven to 350°F.
2. Grease a 12-cup muffin tin and set aside.
3. Heat the oil in a frying pan, add the green onions, and cook over medium heat for 3–4 minutes until they begin to soften.
4. Add the peas and spinach and cook for another 2–3 minutes.
5. Beat the eggs and milk together in a bowl and season with salt and pepper to taste.
6. Divide the pea and spinach mixture between each cup in the muffin tin, then pour some egg and milk mixture over each one.
7. Sprinkle the cheese over the top of each frittata.
8. Bake for 18–20 minutes until golden and set. Leave the frittatas to cool in the dish for a few minutes, then remove them with a spatula to serve.

## Peas in a Pod

Peas grow inside a pod—you can eat them right out of the pod, too!

Did you know peas are actually a fruit? They're considered a fruit because they have seeds and they grow from the female part of a flower called the ovary.

# Strawberry Granola Cups

**Makes:** 2
**Prep:** 5–10 mins

**Ingredients**

½ cup store-bought granola
1 orange, halved
½ cup plain Greek yogurt
1 apple, cored and coarsely grated
½ cup **strawberries**, hulled and sliced
¼ cup blueberries

1. Split most of the granola between two glasses or bowls. Save a little of the granola to use as a garnish on top.
2. Squeeze an orange half into each glass.
3. In a small bowl, mix the yogurt with the grated apple. Then evenly spoon the yogurt mixture over the granola.
4. Top each glass with strawberries and blueberries, then sprinkle with the rest of the granola.

# Let's Pick Strawberries!

Strawberry picking is a fun summer activity! Here are some tips for picking the best strawberries:

Look for firm and fully red berries—those will be tastiest!

Strawberries grow on plants on the ground. The best way to pick a strawberry is to hold the stem just above the berry, gently twist, and pull.

Don't overpack or overfill your berry basket. Only pick the berries you plan to eat or keep, otherwise it's wasteful.

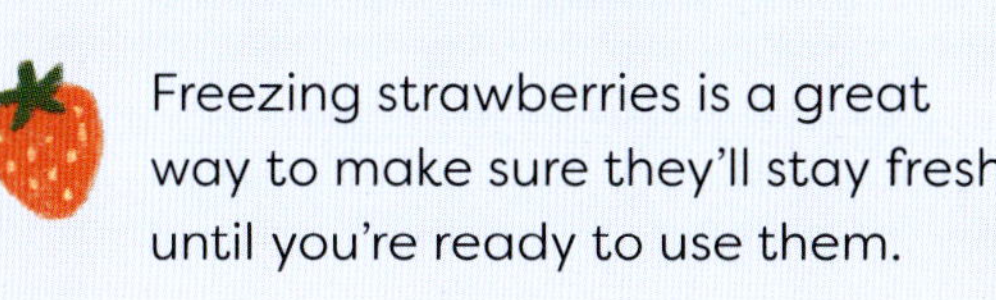

Freezing strawberries is a great way to make sure they'll stay fresh until you're ready to use them.

# Kitchen Herb Garden

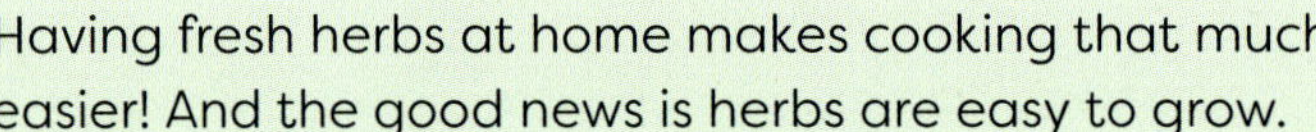

Having fresh herbs at home makes cooking that much easier! And the good news is herbs are easy to grow.

**What You'll Need**

- pot, 6" depth, can drain from the bottom
- potting soil
- garden shovel
- herbs of choice, as seeds or small plants from a nursery
- water
- a place with good sunlight, like a windowsill

1. Use your garden shovel to fill your pot with planting soil a little more than halfway.
2. Place your seeds or plants into the soil and cover to the top with more soil. Press the soil down gently to make sure there is no air around the seed or roots.
3. Water based on what each herb requires.
4. Place the pot somewhere that gets good sunlight, like a windowsill. Herbs should get at least 6 hours of sunlight a day.

### Tip

If you are starting with seeds, be sure to keep the soil consistently moist and water frequently. You may also try putting some plastic wrap or a clear plastic lid over the top of the pot to keep in the moisture. Once the seeds sprout, you can remove the plastic.

# Chive Scrambled Egg Toasts

**Makes:** 4
**Prep:** 10 mins
**Cook:** 6–8 mins

**Ingredients**

4 eggs
½ cup heavy cream
2 tablespoons fresh **chives**, chopped
2 tablespoons butter
4 slices bread, lightly toasted
4 whole fresh chives, to garnish
salt and pepper, to taste

1. Gently whisk together the eggs and cream in a medium-size bowl. Season with salt, pepper, and the chopped chives.
2. In a sauté pan over low heat, melt the butter.
3. Pour in the egg mixture. Let the mixture set slightly, then slowly stir the mixture using a wooden spoon or rubber spatula. The eggs will start to cook. Keep doing this until the eggs are scrambled but still creamy.
4. Place the slices of toast on two plates, then put the scrambled eggs on top of the toasts. Garnish with the whole chives.

# Breakfast Burrito

**Makes:** 1
**Prep:** 15–20 mins
**Cook:** 8–10 mins

**Ingredients**

vegetable oil spray, for greasing
2 eggs
pinch of salt
¼ teaspoon pepper
1 green onion, thinly sliced
½ red or green pepper, diced
2 tablespoons canned **black beans**, rinsed
1 flour tortilla, warmed
1 tablespoon feta cheese, crumbled
2 tablespoons fresh salsa
1 teaspoon cilantro, finely chopped

1. In a small bowl, combine the eggs, salt, pepper, and green onion. Stir well.
2. Spray a nonstick frying pan with vegetable oil and place it over medium-high heat.
3. Add the red pepper and stir for about 3 minutes until it begins to soften.
4. Lower to medium heat, then pour in the egg mixture. Stir often for another 1–2 minutes until the eggs scramble.
5. Put the beans in a microwave-safe bowl and microwave on high for about 1 minute until heated through.
6. Put the scrambled eggs on the tortilla. Top with the beans, cheese, salsa, and chopped cilantro. Fold into a burrito.

BLACK BEANS

GREEN BEANS

CHICKPEAS OR GARBANZO BEANS

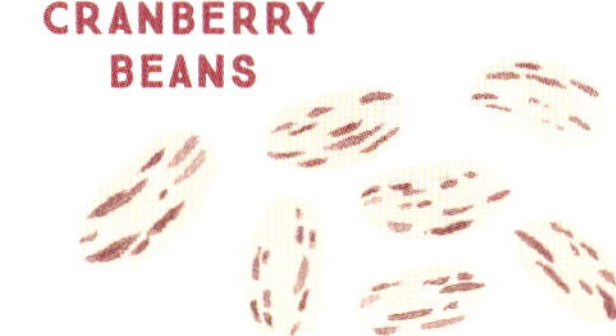

CRANBERRY BEANS

RED BEANS

## Beans, Beans...

There are hundreds of bean varieties in the world. They grow best in warm weather with lots of sun, which is why they're most commonly farmed in Central and South America.

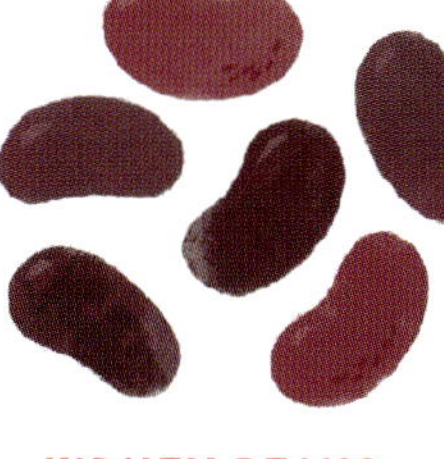

KIDNEY BEANS

PINTO BEANS

BLACK-EYED PEAS

LIMA BEANS

SOYBEANS OR EDAMAME

NAVY BEANS

CANNELLINI BEANS

North Dakota produces the most beans in the United States.

# Juicy Blueberry Facts

One blueberry bush can grow 6,000 blueberries each year!

Blueberries are some of the most antioxidant-rich berries in the world. Antioxidants are vitamins and minerals that keep you healthy.

**Anthocyanin** (an-thow-sai-uh-nin) is the compound that gives blueberries their blue color. Blueberries are one of the only foods in the world that are naturally blue.

**Tip**

Use frozen blueberries if you can't get fresh—stir them into the mixture while still frozen to avoid color bleed.

# Blueberry Scones

**Makes:** 8
**Prep:** 15–20 mins
**Bake:** 18–20 mins

**Ingredients**

1¼ cups all-purpose flour, plus extra for dusting
2 teaspoons baking powder
¼ teaspoon salt
6 tablespoons butter, chilled, plus extra for greasing and to serve
⅓ cup granulated sugar
½ cup **blueberries**
1 egg
½ cup buttermilk
1 tablespoon milk
1 tablespoon demerara sugar

1. Preheat the oven to 400°F.
2. Lightly grease a large baking sheet.
3. Sift together the flour, baking powder, and salt into a bowl. Cut the butter into pieces and mix in until the mixture resembles fine breadcrumbs. Stir in the granulated sugar and blueberries.
4. Beat together the egg and buttermilk, then pour into the bowl. Mix until a soft dough forms.
5. Put some flour on a work surface, like a kitchen counter or table, so the dough doesn't stick. Knead it gently, then shape into a 7-inch-wide circle.
6. Cut the circle into 8 wedges and transfer to the baking sheet. Brush the tops of the wedges with milk and sprinkle with demerara sugar.
7. Bake for 18–20 minutes until risen and golden brown. Transfer to a wire rack to cool, then serve with butter.

3

4

6

# Banana & Berry Acai Bowls

**Serves** 4
**Prep:** 8 mins, plus freezing & cooling
**Cook:** 8–10 mins

**Ingredients**

2 bananas, sliced
2 cups **raspberries**, reserve some for topping
2 cups **blueberries**, reserve some for topping
1 cup rolled oats
2 tablespoons dried **cranberries**
1 tablespoon sunflower seeds
3 tablespoons maple syrup
½ cup milk
1 tablespoon **acai** powder

1. Place the banana slices, raspberries, and blueberries in a single layer on a tray. Freeze for at least 2 hours.
2. Preheat a broiler to medium-hot. Mix the oats, cranberries, sunflower seeds, and maple syrup together, and then spread evenly on a baking sheet.
3. Cook under the preheated broiler for 8–10 minutes, turning frequently, until golden. Watch carefully—it can burn easily! Let cool.
4. Add half of the frozen raspberries, blueberries, and banana slices to a food processer with ¼ cup of milk. Process until mixed together. With the machine running slowly, add the acai powder, then the remaining frozen raspberries, blueberries, and banana slices. Then add the remaining ¼ cup of milk until the mixture is smooth.
5. Divide the mixture among four bowls, top with reserved fresh berries, and sprinkle with the maple-toasted oats.

**Tip**

Almond, coconut, soy, oat, and rice milk are all fantastic nondairy milks that you could use to make these bowls, too.

Scientists have proven that **blackberries** have antioxidants that can help our brain health, especially as we get older.

GOJI BERRIES

BLUEBERRIES

BOYSENBERRIES

## Berries are so good for us!

They contain potassium, magnesium, vitamins C and K, fiber, and more—all things that keep us healthy.

HUCKLEBERRIES

ACAI

MULBERRIES

**Strawberries** are extremely high in vitamin C. Just a few strawberries have the same amount of vitamin C as an orange.

SERVICEBERRIES

# Raspberry, Chia Seed & Pecan Pots

**Makes:** 4
**Prep:** 10 mins

**Ingredients**

1¾ cups **raspberries**
2 tablespoons chia seeds
1 mango, stoned, peeled, and chopped
1¾ cups plain Greek yogurt
3 kiwis, peeled and sliced
pecans, toasted and chopped, to garnish

## Did you know...

There are more than 200 types of raspberries!

A single raspberry has more than 100 seeds.

1. Place the raspberries in a food processor and blend until smooth, then place in a bowl.
2. Stir in the chia seeds, cover, and place in the refrigerator for 1–2 hours—the mixture will thicken to a jam-like consistency.
3. Place the mango in a clean food processor and blend until smooth.
4. Pour mango into a bowl and lightly stir in the yogurt, leaving trails of mango showing.
5. Layer the mango-yogurt mixture, raspberry-chia mixture, and kiwi slices in four glasses, finishing with yogurt on top. Garnish with chopped pecans.

The raspberry is part of the same family as a popular flower. Do you know which one? A rose!

ROSE PLANT

RASPBERRY PLANT

FLOWER

THORNS

FRUIT

LEAVES

# Flour's Journey

Flour is made from different grains.

The grain is dried and gets ground into a flour.

The most common type of flour is made from wheat grain, but flour can be made using other grains, nuts, seeds, and rice.

# Cinnamon Buns

**Makes** 8
**Prep:** 10–15 mins
**Bake:** 10–14 mins

**Ingredients**

3 tablespoons brown sugar
3 tablespoons butter, softened, plus extra for greasing
1½ teaspoons ground cinnamon
8 ounces ready-to-bake canned croissants
3 tablespoons confectioners' sugar, sifted
1½ teaspoons lukewarm water

1. Preheat the oven to 400°F.
2. Lightly grease 8 cups of a muffin tin.
3. Beat together the sugar, butter, and cinnamon until smooth.
4. Unroll the croissant dough but don't separate it into triangles. Spread the cinnamon butter along the length of the croissant dough.
5. Gently roll up the dough from one short side. Using a sharp knife, slice the roll into 8 rounds.
6. Place 1 round, flat-side down, in each of the 8 cups in the prepared tin, pressing down gently.
7. Bake for 10–14 minutes until risen and golden.
8. Meanwhile, mix the confectioners' sugar and water in a small bowl to make a smooth icing.
9. Leave the buns to cool in the dish for 1–2 minutes, then transfer to a wire rack. Using a teaspoon, drizzle the icing over the hot buns.

# Where Does Chocolate Come From?

To make chocolate, pods from the cacao tree are needed. There are about 40 seeds inside each pod.

The seeds are dried and roasted to make cocoa beans. Then the hard skin is taken off each bean. Next, the cocoa beans are ground into a paste.

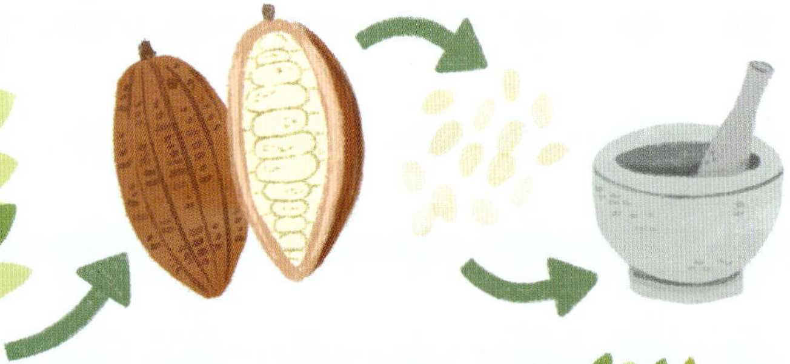

Chocolatiers (chocolate makers) mix in butter, milk, sugar, and sometimes other flavorings to make chocolate we eat!

# Waffles with Bananas and Chocolate Hazelnut Spread

**Makes:** 6
**Prep:** 10 mins
**Cook:** 18–30 mins

**Ingredients**

nonstick cooking spray
2 large eggs
2 cups all-purpose flour
1¾ cups milk
½ cup vegetable oil
1 tablespoon granulated sugar
4 teaspoons baking powder
¼ teaspoon salt
½ teaspoon vanilla extract
2 bananas, sliced, for serving
chocolate hazelnut spread, for serving

1. Preheat the waffle iron.
2. In a large bowl, whisk together eggs until they're light and fluffy.
3. Mix in flour, milk, and oil.
4. Add sugar, then baking powder, salt, and vanilla. Don't mix too much.
5. Spray the waffle iron with nonstick spray. Pour about ⅓ cup of batter on the iron, close the top, and cook until the iron stops steaming. This usually takes 3–5 minutes.
6. Gently remove the cooked waffle from the iron. Repeat until the batter is gone, spraying the iron each time batter is poured. Serve with sliced bananas and chocolate hazelnut spread (see page 28).

# Chocolate Hazelnut Spread

Makes: 8 ounces
Prep: 15 mins, plus standing
Cook: 3–4 mins

**Ingredients**

½ cup unblanched **hazelnuts**
2 tablespoons raw cacao powder or unsweetened cocoa powder
⅓ cup brown sugar
½ cup olive oil
½ teaspoon vanilla extract
pinch of sea salt
toast, pancakes, or waffles, to serve (optional)

**Tip**

Most nuts would work in this recipe—try replacing the hazelnuts with the same quantity of almonds for a tasty twist.

1. Add the hazelnuts to a dry pan and cook over medium heat for 3–4 minutes, constantly shaking the pan, until the nuts are an even golden brown color.
2. Wrap the nuts in a clean tea towel and rub to remove the skins.
3. Put the nuts in a food processor and blend until finely ground.
4. Add the cacao powder, sugar, oil, vanilla extract, and salt, and blend to make a smooth paste.
5. Spoon the paste into a small jar and cover. Keep it at room temperature for 4 hours, until the sugar has dissolved completely.
6. Stir again, then store in the refrigerator for up to 5 days. Serve on toast, pancakes, or waffles.

## That's Nuts!

Some foods that we think of as nuts are actually "drupes." Drupes are fruits that are fleshy on the outside and contain a shell covering a seed on the inside.

CASHEW

# How Do Cranberries Grow?

Cranberries grow in beds called bogs. A bog is made of spongy, acidic ground and plants, usually in an open body of water.

Some cranberries grow on vines in the bog. When they're ready to be harvested, farmers use water reels to churn the water to loosen the berries from the vines. They float to the surface of the bog and are collected. This is called wet harvesting.

Sometimes farmers dry harvest cranberries. Dry harvesting is when the bog is drained and machinery is used to pick cranberries from the vines. The berries are collected in sacks at the back of the machine.

# Cranberry-Orange-Walnut Bread

**Makes:** 1 loaf, 16 servings
**Prep:** 20 mins
**Bake:** 1 hr

**Ingredients**

2 cups all-purpose flour
1 cup granulated sugar
1½ teaspoons baking powder
1 teaspoon baking soda
½ teaspoon salt
1 large egg
½ cup orange juice
zest of 1 orange
2 tablespoons butter, melted, plus extra for greasing
2 tablespoons hot water
1 cup fresh or frozen **cranberries**
1 cup walnuts, chopped

1. Preheat the oven to 325°F.
2. In a large bowl, mix together flour, sugar, baking powder, baking soda, and salt.
3. In another bowl, beat the egg until light and fluffy.
4. Add the egg, orange juice, zest, melted butter, and hot water to the dry ingredients.
5. Gently mix in the cranberries and walnuts.
6. Pour into a greased 9x5-inch loaf pan. Bake until a toothpick inserted in the center comes out clean, about 1 hour.
7. Leave to cool for 10 minutes before removing from pan and placing on a wire rack to cool completely.

# Planting a Bean Seed

Do you ever wonder what plants look like underground? Try this bean seed experiment to see how roots grow.

**What You'll Need**

- 1 bean seed
- paper towel
- resealable plastic bag
- water

1. Fold the paper towel in half, wet it, and wring it out gently. Place it flat in the plastic bag.
2. Place the bean seed on top of the paper towel in the bag.
3. Seal the bag and put it in a sunny location. You could even tape it to a window as long as you can see the seed.

4. Now wait. You might see roots sprout overnight, or it may take up to 5 days. When you see green shoots or leaves, the seed is ready to move to soil. Or you can let the plant grow longer in the bag by unsealing it and wetting the paper towel a little bit more.

   If you do plant your bean seed in soil, now you will know how the roots grow down while the plant grows up!

# Farmers Markets

A farmers market is an outdoor market where farmers and small businesses sell their crops and products, like fruits and vegetables, meat, cheese, coffee, baked goods, plants, and homemade items like soap. These markets are a great way to connect with local farmers and businesses!

One of the first recorded farmers markets in North America was in Boston in 1634.

LUNCH

# Spring Rolls
## with Coconut Dip

**Makes:** 16 half-rolls, serves 4
**Prep:** 15 mins

**Ingredients**

8 round rice spring roll wrappers
1 yellow bell pepper, halved, seeded, and thinly sliced
1 red bell pepper, halved, seeded, and thinly sliced
½ cucumber, halved, seeded, and thinly sliced
1 bok choy, leaves separated and stalks sliced
2 carrots, peeled and cut into 4-inch sticks
4 large green onions, sliced lengthwise
2 celery stalks, thinly sliced lengthwise
2 teaspoons **coconut** aminos

1. Soak a spring roll wrapper in a shallow bowl of water for 10 seconds, or until just pliable, then smooth it on a cutting board.
2. Arrange one-eighth of the raw vegetables on the lower center of the wrap. Sprinkle with a little of the coconut aminos.
3. Tuck each side of the wrapper into the center, then fold the lower edge up to enclose the vegetables, keeping them in a tight bunch as you roll up to the top. Repeat with the other seven wrappers.
4. Cut each roll in half until you have 16 pieces. Arrange on a serving dish with a bowl of dip.

# Inside a Coconut

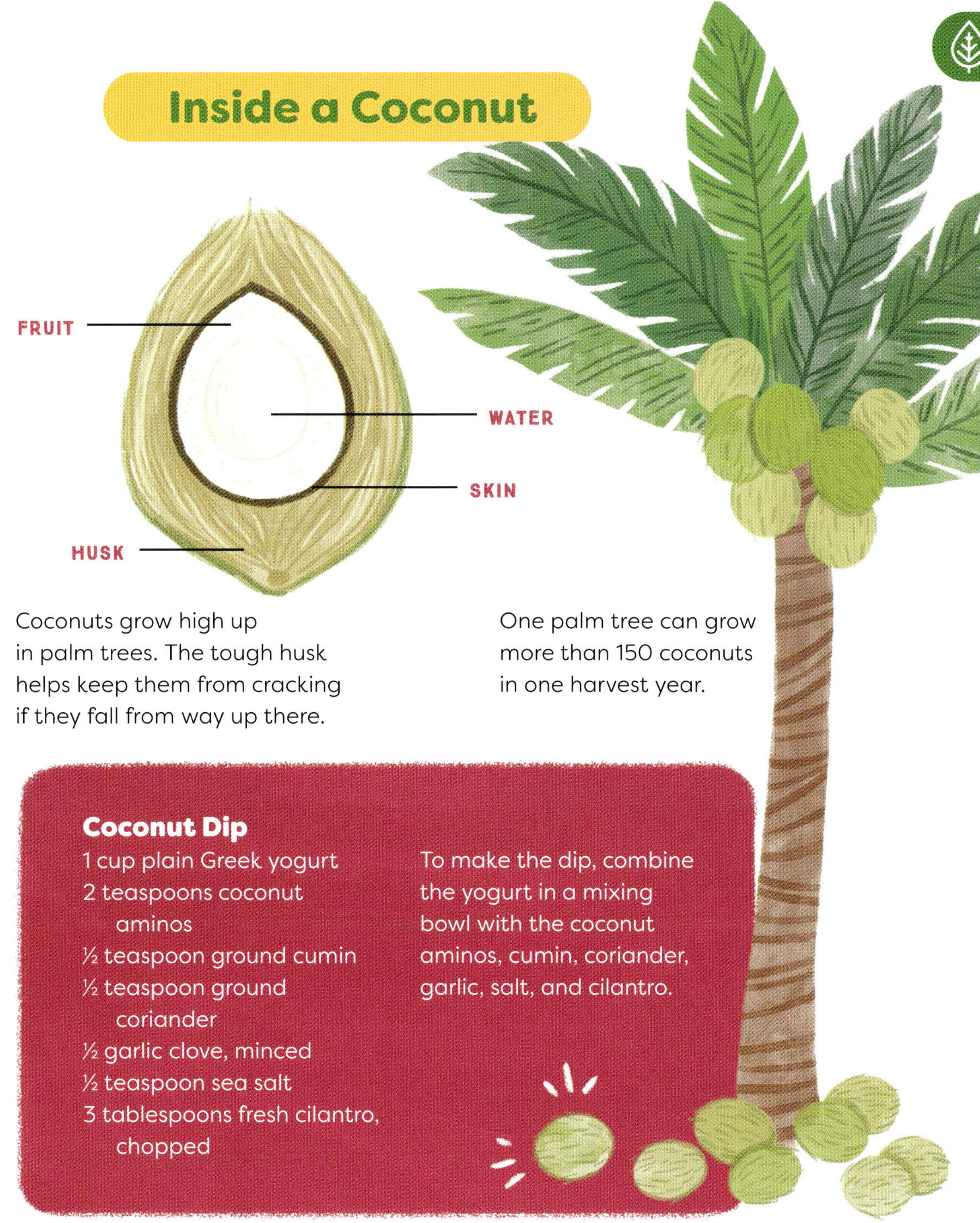


Coconuts grow high up in palm trees. The tough husk helps keep them from cracking if they fall from way up there.

One palm tree can grow more than 150 coconuts in one harvest year.

### Coconut Dip

- 1 cup plain Greek yogurt
- 2 teaspoons coconut aminos
- ½ teaspoon ground cumin
- ½ teaspoon ground coriander
- ½ garlic clove, minced
- ½ teaspoon sea salt
- 3 tablespoons fresh cilantro, chopped

To make the dip, combine the yogurt in a mixing bowl with the coconut aminos, cumin, coriander, garlic, salt, and cilantro.

# Fried Mozzarella Sticks with Homemade Ranch Dip

**Makes:** 12
**Prep:** 20 mins
**Cook:** 10 mins

**Ingredients**

2 large eggs, beaten
¼ cup water
1½ cups Italian-style seasoned bread crumbs
½ teaspoon garlic salt
⅔ cup all-purpose flour
⅓ cup cornstarch
oil for frying, as needed
1 (12-ounce) package **mozzarella cheese** sticks

1. In a bowl, mix together the flour and cornstarch.
2. In another bowl, whisk together the water and eggs.
3. In a third bowl, mix together the bread crumbs and garlic salt.
4. Take a mozzarella stick and roll it in the flour and cornstarch mixture, shaking off any extra.
5. Next, dip it in the egg and water mixture.
6. Then press it into the bread crumbs until it's covered entirely. Repeat with the other mozzarella sticks.
7. Place coated mozzarella sticks on a baking sheet and put in the freezer before frying, at least 30 minutes.
8. In a heavy saucepan, heat oil to 365°F.
9. Using a pair of tongs, carefully lower a few cheese sticks into the hot oil.
10. Fry until golden brown, about 30 seconds.
11. Remove cheese sticks from the oil using the tongs and drain on a paper towel. Repeat with the rest of the cheese sticks.
12. Serve warm with the homemade ranch dip.

## Did you know?

Mozzarella is made from cow's milk, and so are many other types of cheese and dairy products!

CHEDDAR

BRIE

SWISS

BLUE

### Homemade Ranch Dip

¼ cup Italian parsley, chopped
2 tablespoons fresh chives, chopped
1 cup mayonnaise
½ cup sour cream
buttermilk, as needed to reach desired consistency
salt and pepper, to taste

To make the ranch dip, mix together all ingredients in a small bowl. Season with salt and pepper to taste. Chill for a few hours before serving.

# Egg-cellent Egg Facts

Farm-fresh eggs come in different shades of colors, but they all taste the same! An egg's color is determined by the type of chicken that lays the egg.

One chicken can lay about 250 eggs each year!

# Deviled Eggs

**Makes:** 16
**Prep:** 20–25 mins, plus cooling
**Cook:** 10 mins

**Ingredients**

8 large **eggs**
5 tablespoons mayonnaise
1½ teaspoons yellow mustard
1½ teaspoons white vinegar
1 teaspoon paprika, to garnish
fresh parsley, to garnish
salt and pepper, to taste

1. Put the eggs in a saucepan, cover with cold water, and slowly bring to a boil.
2. Lower the heat to very low, cover, and simmer gently for 10 minutes.
3. Drain the eggs and place under cold running water until they are cold. Crack the eggshells and remove.
4. Halve the eggs lengthwise. Carefully remove the yolks and place them in a sieve set over a bowl. Rub them through the sieve, then mash with a fork.
5. Add the mayonnaise, mix together well, then add the mustard and white vinegar, and season with salt and pepper.
6. Use a spoon to put a little of the egg yolk mixture in the hollow of each egg white half.
7. Arrange the eggs on a platter to serve. Dust with a little paprika and parsley.

1

4

4

# Avocado & Sweet Corn Salad

**Makes:** 4 servings
**Prep:** 20 mins
**Cook:** 5 mins

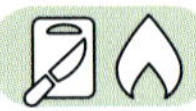

**Ingredients**

1 cup fresh **sweet corn** (or frozen sweet corn, thawed)
1 large avocado, halved, stoned, peeled, and cut into cubes
¾ cup cherry tomatoes, cut into quarters
½ red onion, finely chopped
1 small green pepper, halved, seeded, and cut into small chunks
3 leaves of kale, shredded
1 tablespoon fresh cilantro, roughly chopped

**Dressing**

zest and juice of 1 lime
2 tablespoons olive oil
salt and pepper, to taste

1. Bring water to a boil in a saucepan.
2. Add the sweet corn and simmer for 3 minutes.
3. Drain into a colander, rinse with cold water, drain again, then transfer to a salad bowl.
4. To make the dressing, put the lime zest, juice, and oil in a jar, screw on the lid, and shake well. Season to taste with salt and pepper.
5. Add the avocado, tomatoes, onion, green pepper, kale, and cilantro to the sweet corn.
6. Drizzle with the dressing and toss together, then spoon into four bowls.

# Grow, Corn, Grow!

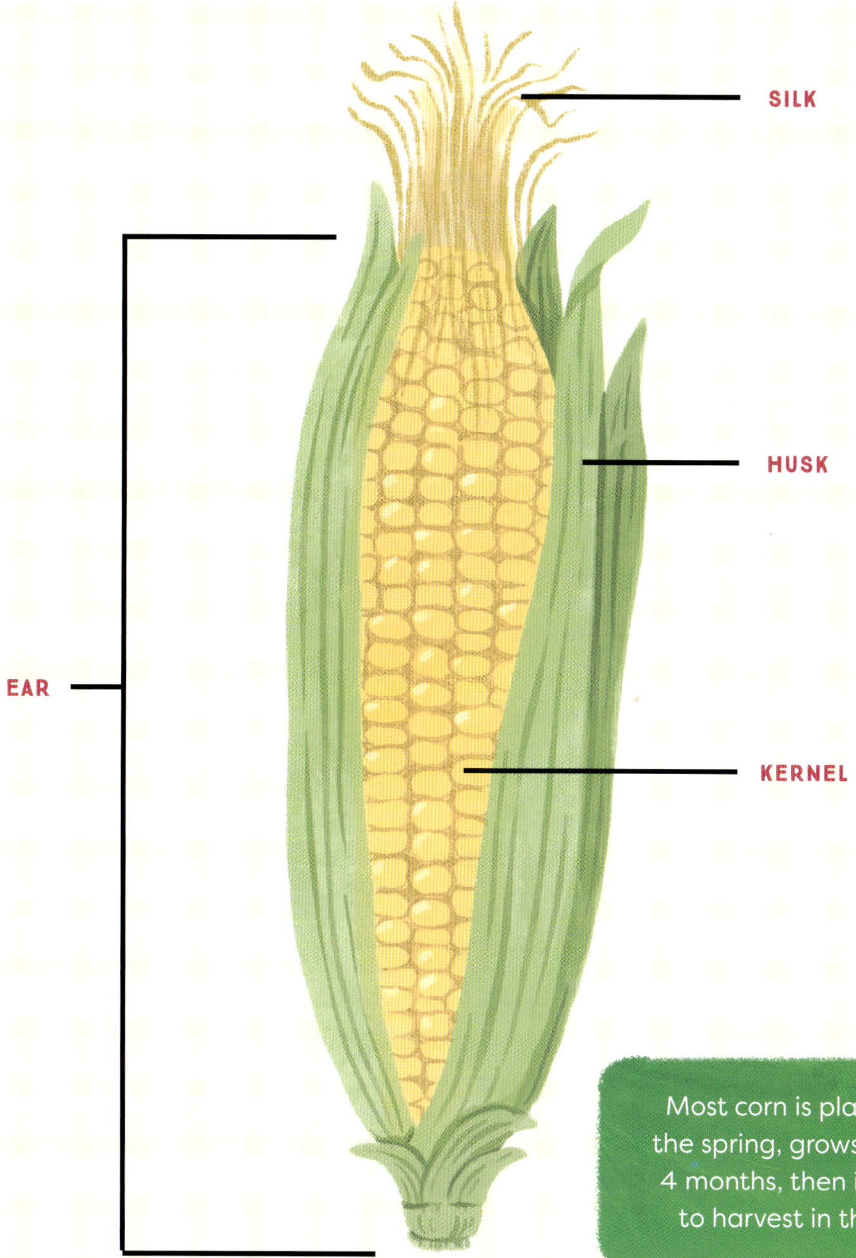

SILK

HUSK

EAR

KERNEL

Most corn is planted in the spring, grows for 3 to 4 months, then is ready to harvest in the fall.

# Mini Corn Dog Muffins

**Makes:** 24
**Prep:** 20 mins
**Bake:** 18–20 mins

**Ingredients**

nonstick cooking spray
½ cup butter, melted
½ cup sugar
2 eggs
1 cup buttermilk
½ teaspoon baking soda
1 cup **cornmeal**
1 cup all-purpose flour
½ teaspoon salt
8 all-beef hot dogs, cut into 1-inch bites

1. Preheat the oven to 375°F.
2. In a large bowl, whisk together the butter and sugar.
3. Add eggs to the butter and sugar mixture and mix.
4. Add buttermilk and whisk together.
5. In another bowl, mix together the baking soda, cornmeal, flour, and salt. Add the dry mixture into the wet mixture.
6. Spray a 24-cup mini muffin tin with nonstick cooking spray. Pour the batter into your muffin tin, filling each cup two-thirds of the way up, then add one hot dog bite into the middle of each cup.
7. Bake for 18–20 minutes or until cornbread is golden brown.
8. Let cool in the muffin tin for a few minutes before serving.

Serve hot with baked beans, french fries, or roasted broccoli (see page 83). Or eat them on their own with some ketchup and mustard!

EKCO
080
CHICAGO

# Cool Cucumber Rolls

**Makes:** 8 rolls, serves 4
**Prep:** 25 mins

**Cucumber Rolls**

1 (12-inch-long) **cucumber**
¾ cup cauliflower florets
1 teaspoon sesame oil
1 teaspoon rice vinegar
½ teaspoon salt
½ avocado, halved and stoned
2 green onions, finely chopped
½ small red bell pepper, thinly sliced
sea salt, to taste

1. Cut off the ends of the cucumber so there's a center section that is one width.
2. Cut into eight pieces, each 1½ inches long.
3. Scoop out the seeds and about half the flesh from each piece to form eight hollow rolls.
4. Put the cauliflower, sesame oil, rice vinegar, and salt into a food processor, and pulse until the mixture resembles cooked rice.
5. Mash the avocado in a small bowl, adding sea salt to taste.
6. Arrange your cucumber rolls on a board or serving plate and fill each one with some cauliflower rice, pressing it toward the sides.
7. Add some avocado next to the cauliflower rice. Tuck the peppers and green onions into the middle of each roll. Serve with Spicy Cashew Dip (see page 47).

**Spicy Cashew Dip**

½ cup raw cashew nuts, soaked in water for 1 hour, drained, and rinsed
2 teaspoons finely chopped fresh ginger
2 teaspoons wasabi paste

To make the dip, put the soaked nuts into a food processor and process for several minutes until you have a creamy consistency. Add in the ginger and wasabi paste, then transfer to a small serving dish.

## Cool Cucumbers

Cucumbers are in the same family as gourds, melons, and pumpkins.

**Some cucumbers have little hairs on the outside. And some have tiny spikes—be careful when picking them!**

# Pizza Pancakes

**Makes:** 8
**Prep:** 15 mins
**Cook:** 10 mins

**Ingredients**

nonstick cooking spray
2 cups biscuit mix
2 teaspoons Italian seasoning
2 eggs
1 cup milk
½ cup part-skim mozzarella cheese, shredded
½ cup pepperoni, chopped
¼ cup **cherry tomatoes**, seeded and chopped
¼ cup green peppers, chopped
1 cup pizza sauce, warmed, for dipping

1. In a large bowl, mix together the biscuit mix and Italian seasoning.
2. In another bowl, whisk together eggs and milk until light and fluffy.
3. Add the egg mixture to the dry ingredients and mix together.
4. Gently stir in the cheese, pepperoni, tomatoes, and peppers.
5. Preheat a griddle to medium heat. Spray with nonstick cooking spray.
6. Pour ¼ cup of batter on the griddle. Cook until bubbles start to form on the top and the bottoms turn golden brown. Flip and cook until the other side is golden brown. Repeat steps 5 and 6 until the batter is gone.
7. Serve with pizza sauce for dipping.

Anybody can grow cherry tomatoes, no matter how much space they have. All you need is a pot and some sunshine. Place the tomato plant in a window that gets bright, direct sun, and water it often. When flowers appear, gently shake the plant to help it pollinate.

# Eating the Rainbow

Eating a wide variety of foods in different colors means you're getting nutrients that keep your body healthy and growing. How many colorful, fresh foods can you think of? Here are some ideas:

watermelon, tomato, strawberry, bell pepper, cherry, pomegranate, apple

carrot, apricot, sweet potato, squash, orange, pumpkin, cantaloupe, tangerine

pineapple, banana, lemon, corn, mango, summer squash

lettuce, green bean, cucumber, avocado, zucchini, spinach, kale, kiwi, pear

blueberry, elderberry, currant

grape, eggplant, taro, beet, cabbage

Different types of colored chard grouped together is called rainbow chard. The stalks can be yellow, pink, white, or red.

# Turkey & Rainbow Chard Roll-ups

**Makes:** 8 rolls
**Prep:** 30 mins

**Ingredients**

8 **rainbow chard** leaves and stems (choose leaves that are about the same size as the slices of turkey)
1 avocado, halved and stoned
juice of 1 lemon
8 thin slices deli turkey
⅔ cup hummus
2 green onions, trimmed and cut into fine strips
1 carrot, cut into matchstick strips
1 small zucchini, cut into matchstick strips

1. Cut the stems from the chard leaves, then cut the stems into matchstick strips and set aside.
2. Peel the avocado and cut into long, thin slices, then toss in the lemon juice and set aside.
3. Separate the chard leaves and arrange, shiny-side down, on a large chopping board.
4. Cover each one with a slice of turkey, then spread the turkey with a little hummus.
5. Divide the chard stems, green onions, carrot, and zucchini between the chard leaves.
6. Make a little pile on each leaf that runs through the center of the leaf, from long edge to long edge.
7. Top the little mounds with the avocado slices, then roll up from the base of the leaf to the tip and put on a plate, seam downward. Continue until all the leaves have been rolled, then cut each roll into thick slices.

1

6

7

# Mushroom & Cheese Quesadillas

**Makes:** 5
**Prep:** 10 mins
**Cook:** 10 mins

**Ingredients**

2 tablespoons olive oil
1 pound **mushrooms**, thickly sliced
1 clove garlic, finely chopped
½ bunch green onions, thinly sliced
¼ teaspoon salt
⅛ teaspoon ground black pepper
1½ cups grated cheddar or Monterey Jack
fresh cilantro leaves, chopped
10 (6-inch) flour tortillas
salsa, optional, to serve
jalapeños, optional, to serve

1. Add oil to a large pan over medium-high heat.
2. Once the oil is hot, add the mushrooms and cook for 5 minutes, stirring a few times.
3. Add the garlic and green onions to the pan and cook for 2–4 minutes until you can smell the garlic. Add salt and pepper. Remove from heat.
4. Put a tortilla in a clean pan over medium heat. Put 2 tablespoons of cheese and 2 tablespoons of mushrooms on top. Add chopped cilantro and another 2 tablespoons of cheese.
5. Put another tortilla on top and press down lightly.
6. Cook for about 1 minute or until the cheese starts to melt.
7. Flip using a large spatula and cook on the other side for another 30 seconds. The tortillas should start to get brown and toasty.
8. Do this with the rest of the tortillas and filling. Serve with salsa and jalapeños if desired.

There are 14,000 types of mushrooms in the world. About 70–80 of those species are poisonous, which is why it's important to never eat any wild mushrooms you may find in nature.

PORTOBELLO

SHIITAKE

ENOKI

OYSTER

## Mushrooms Are Cool...

They're the biggest living thing on our planet. They can grow for miles underground. The largest is a honey mushroom that measures 3.5 miles long and is 2,400 years old!

MOREL

CHANTERELLE

PORCINI

**Did you know mushrooms aren't vegetables? They're an organism called fungi.**

Some mushrooms can glow in the dark! Scientists believe there are around 80 different types of mushrooms that can glow.

# Brussels Sprouts Mac & Cheese

**Makes:** 6 servings
**Prep:** 10 mins
**Cook:** 20 mins

**Ingredients**

8 ounces cavatappi, or any preferred pasta
1 tablespoon olive oil or butter
1 pound **brussels sprouts**, halved and any outer yellow leaves removed
½ teaspoon garlic powder
2 tablespoons butter
2 cloves garlic, minced
¼ cup all-purpose flour
1¾ cups milk
2 cups cheddar cheese, shredded, reserve some to garnish
salt and pepper, to taste

1. Cook pasta according to the directions on the package, then drain and set aside.
2. Add oil to a large pot over medium-high heat. When the oil is hot, add the brussels sprouts and garlic powder.
3. Stir often and cook until brussels sprouts start to turn golden brown. When cooked, put the brussels sprouts in a bowl and set aside.
4. To make the cheese sauce, put butter and garlic in a large pot over medium-high heat. When the butter is melted, add in flour and whisk until a paste forms.

5. Slowly add in milk, constantly stirring to remove any lumps.
6. Increase heat and bring mixture to a boil, then reduce heat and simmer for a few minutes, stirring every so often until sauce begins to thicken.
7. Add cheese and stir until it's completely melted. Add salt and pepper to taste.
8. Add the pasta and brussels sprouts to the cheese sauce and stir to combine.
9. Scoop mac and cheese into bowls and serve with more cheese.

## Brussels Sprout Tidbits

Brussels sprouts grow on strong stalks that can be 2 to 3 feet tall. When they're ready to be picked, you twist and pull from the stalk.

They belong to the same family as cabbage, which is why they look like tiny cabbages.

# What's a Leek?

A leek is part of the allium vegetable family, which means they're related to garlic, chives, onions, and shallots. They taste similar to an onion but are a little sweeter in flavor.

LEAF

STEM

ROOT

To prepare a leek for use, slice off the root and the dark green leaves.

Then slice the leek in half lengthwise. Place in a colander and rinse to get rid of any dirt or sandy soil.

For cooking, you can cut leeks into half-moon pieces.

# Leek & Spinach Soup

**Makes:** 4 servings
**Prep:** 20 mins
**Cook:** 45 mins

**Ingredients**

2 tablespoons butter
2 **leeks**, trimmed, halved lengthwise, thoroughly rinsed, and thinly sliced
1 cup potatoes, cut into bite-size chunks
1⅓ cups spinach, stalks discarded, leaves sliced
32 ounces vegetable stock
1 teaspoon lemon juice
pinch of nutmeg
sea salt and pepper, to taste
sour cream, to serve

1. Melt the butter in a large saucepan over medium-low heat.
2. Add the leeks and potatoes, cover, and cook for 10 minutes until beginning to soften.
3. Stir in two-thirds of the spinach. Cover and cook for 2–3 minutes until starting to wilt.
4. Season with salt and pepper, then stir in half the stock. Bring to a boil, then simmer for 20 minutes, partially covered.
5. Transfer half the soup to a food processor and process until smooth. Return to the pan.
6. Puree the remaining uncooked spinach and the remaining stock. Add to the soup in the pan. Stir in the lemon juice and nutmeg and gently reheat.
7. Ladle into bowls and swirl in a spoonful of sour cream.

# Garlic Bread Twists

**Makes:** 15 servings
**Prep:** 10 mins
**Bake:** 8–10 mins

**Ingredients**

1 (1-pound) package premade pizza dough
½ cup butter, melted
2 tablespoons Parmesan cheese, grated
1 tablespoon dried parsley
1 tablespoon **garlic**, minced
1 teaspoon garlic salt
sesame seeds, for sprinkling
cornmeal, for sprinkling

1. Preheat the oven to 450°F.
2. Cut the dough into 15 dough balls of the same size.
3. Roll each ball into a long rope, about 6 inches by 1 inch. You can add a little twist or leave it straight.
4. In a bowl, mix together the melted butter, parsley, garlic, cheese, and garlic salt.
5. Brush the mixture over each piece of dough, then sprinkle with sesame seeds.
6. Sprinkle a baking sheet with some cornmeal, then place the bread sticks on the sheet.
7. Bake for 8–10 minutes minutes or until golden brown.
8. Remove from the oven and coat the twists again with the butter mixture.

# Grow Garlic!

Want to grow garlic? The main thing you need to do is plan ahead. Garlic will be ready to harvest in the summer as long as it is planted the fall before. All you have to do is wait until about 2 weeks after the first hard frost, then take a clove of garlic and plant it in the ground with the stem side up. When it's ready to harvest, that single clove will have multiplied into a beautiful bulb of garlic!

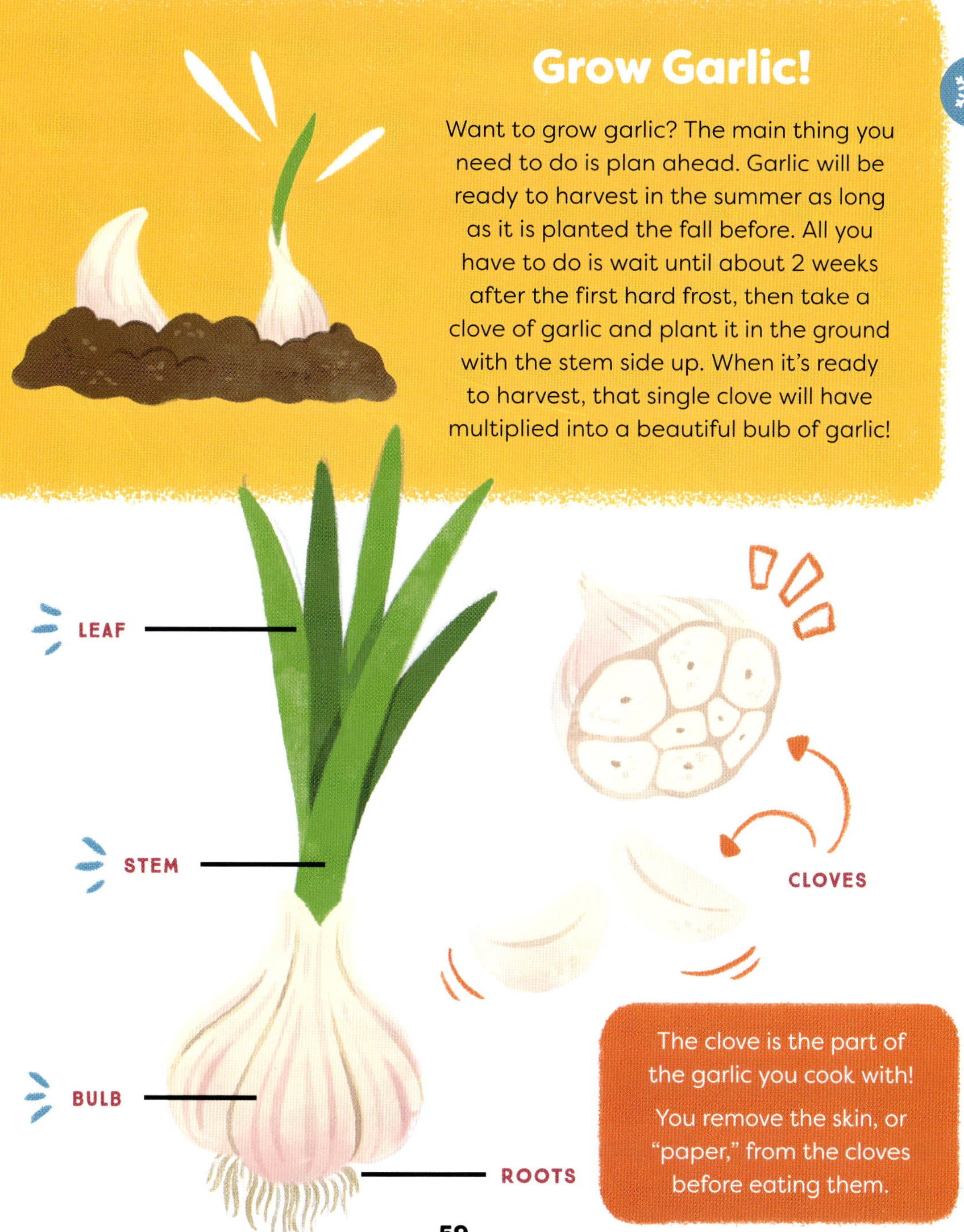


The clove is the part of the garlic you cook with!

You remove the skin, or "paper," from the cloves before eating them.

# Types of Tractors

Compact tractors are great for many uses because of their convenient size. They can be used on small farms for various tasks or to help with landscaping.

Utility tractors are also known as chore tractors. They can help wrangle livestock, remove snow, bale hay, and much more.

Specialty tractors are used when working with specialty crops like grapes in vineyards or apples in orchards.

Row crop tractors help make planting and harvesting easier and faster.

DINNER

# Pizza with Spinach and Bacon

**Makes:** 4 servings
**Prep:** 5 mins
**Bake:** 5–10 mins

**Ingredients**

1 prebaked 12-inch pizza crust
⅓ cup pizza sauce
1 cup mozzarella, shredded
2 cups fresh baby **spinach**, thinly sliced
1 cup bacon crumbles
Italian seasoning, optional, to serve

1. Preheat the oven to 450°F.
2. Put crust on an ungreased baking sheet.
3. Spread the pizza sauce over the crust.
4. Sprinkle cheese, spinach, and bacon crumbles over the sauce.
5. Bake until the cheese has melted and the crust is golden brown, about 5–10 minutes. Sprinkle Italian seasoning, if using, to serve.

## Amazing Spinach

The word "spinach" comes from the Persian word "ispanai," which means "green hand."

In the Middle Ages, artists extracted the green pigment from spinach and used it to make ink for their art.

# All About Asparagus

After an asparagus seed is planted, it will take 3 years before it's ready to be picked. After its initial picking, you can continue to pick it each year.

Asparagus gets its name from the Greek word "asparagos," which means "sprout" or "shoot."

# Asparagus Wrapped in Prosciutto

**Makes:** 4 servings
**Prep:** 10 mins
**Bake:** 10 mins

**Ingredients**

1 pound **asparagus**
1 tablespoon olive oil
⅛ teaspoon salt
⅛ teaspoon freshly ground black pepper
½ pound thinly sliced prosciutto
1 ounce Parmigiano Reggiano cheese, grated

1. Preheat the oven to 425°F.
2. Cut the tough ends off the asparagus.
3. Put the asparagus on a baking sheet, drizzle with olive oil, salt, and pepper, and toss to make sure the spears are fully covered.
4. Put the prosciutto slices on a cutting board. Slice each piece in half.
5. Add a thin layer of cheese over all the prosciutto.
6. Roll each asparagus spear with a piece of prosciutto.
7. Arrange all the spears on the baking sheet.
8. Bake for about 10 minutes. The asparagus will be tender but firm.
9. Serve with more cheese on top.

# Cheesy Sweet Corn Fritters

**Makes:** 8 fritters
**Prep:** 15 mins
**Cook:** 3–4 mins

**Ingredients**

1 egg
¾ cup milk
½ cup all-purpose flour
½ teaspoon baking powder
⅓ cup canned sweet corn kernels, drained
4 tablespoons cheddar cheese, grated
1 teaspoon fresh chives, chopped
2 teaspoons oil

1. Put the egg and milk into a medium bowl and beat with a fork.
2. Add the flour and baking powder, and beat until smooth.
3. Stir in the sweet corn, cheese, and chives.
4. Heat the oil in a nonstick frying pan over medium heat. Drop tablespoonfuls of the batter into the pan.
5. Cook for 1–2 minutes until the fritters are puffed up and golden. Flip and cook for another minute on the opposite side.
6. Remove and drain on paper towels before serving.

# How Does Popcorn Pop?

The popcorn we eat starts out as a piece of corn called a kernel. Every kernel has a tiny amount of water inside, along with a hard shell, called a hull, on the outside.

When a kernel gets warm—by heating on the stove or in the microwave—the little bit of water inside turns to steam. That steam creates pressure inside the kernel.

At some point, the hull can't take the pressure anymore! And—POP—a fluffy piece of popcorn is made.

You can season popcorn with lots of flavors! Salt, butter, grated cheese, ranch seasoning, melted caramel or marshmallow, or—if you're a risk taker—a little pepper.

# Fresh Tomato Soup with Pasta

**Makes:** 4 servings
**Prep:** 20 mins
**Cook:** 1 hr 5 mins

**Ingredients**

1 tablespoon olive oil
4 large plum **tomatoes**, diced
1 onion, cut into quarters
1 garlic clove, thinly sliced
1 celery stick, coarsely chopped
2½ cups chicken stock
½ cup dried small pasta, like orzo or ditalini
salt and pepper, to taste
4 teaspoons fresh parsley, chopped, to garnish

1. Pour the oil into a large, heavy-based saucepan and add the tomatoes, onion, garlic, and celery.
2. Cover and cook over low heat, occasionally stirring, for 45 minutes until pulpy.
3. Transfer the mixture to a food processor or blender and process to a smooth puree.
4. Add the puree and stock to a clean saucepan. Bring to a boil.
5. Add the pasta and cook for 8–10 minutes until pasta is tender. Season to taste with salt and pepper.
6. Ladle the soup into bowls and sprinkle with chopped parsley.

ROMA

BETTER BOY

# Terrific Tomatoes

Can you guess how many varieties of tomatoes exist? More than 10,000! That's a lot of tomatoes.

CHEROKEE PURPLE

CHERRY

PLUM

BLACK KRIM

BEEFSTEAK

The most tomatoes ever grown on a single plant in one year was 32,194 tomatoes! The plant weighed more than 1,000 pounds.

# Homemade Pickles

**Makes:** 1 (12-ounce) jar
**Prep:** 15 mins, plus
1+ hrs rest

**Ingredients**

1 medium-to-large cucumber or 2 small cucumbers
½ cup room-temperature water
½ cup rice vinegar
1½ tablespoons maple syrup or sugar
1½ teaspoons fine sea salt
20 twists of freshly ground black pepper
¼ cup fresh dill, chopped
2 cloves garlic, peeled and smashed
1 bay leaf

1. Slice the cucumbers into thin rounds and set aside.
2. Combine water, vinegar, syrup or sugar, salt, and pepper in a bowl. Stir until the salt has dissolved, and set aside.
3. Put the cucumbers in a sterilized wide-mouth jar, along with the dill and garlic on top and the bay leaf tucked into the side.
4. Pour all the liquid over the cucumbers until they're fully covered.
5. Carefully cover the jar and put in the refrigerator for 1 hour minimum, but the flavor will continue to get stronger over the next few days.
6. These pickles will stay fresh in the refrigerator for up to 3 weeks. Eat them by themselves, serve on hamburgers and sandwiches, or bread them to make fried pickles.

# Fried Pickles

**Makes:** 8 servings
**Prep:** 10 mins
**Cook:** 10 mins

**Ingredients**

vegetable oil for frying
½ cup all-purpose flour
1 teaspoon Italian seasoning
1 teaspoon garlic powder
¼ teaspoon salt
¼ teaspoon black pepper
½ cup water
16 ounces jarred dill **pickle** slices, drained and dried

1. Heat 2 inches of vegetable oil in a large pot over medium-high heat until it reaches 375°F.
2. In a bowl, mix together the flour, Italian seasoning, garlic powder, salt, and pepper.
3. Add water and mix until combined.
4. Dip the pickles in the batter and coat well on all sides.
5. Carefully add pickles to the oil one at a time. Fry in small batches for 1–2 minutes on each side until golden brown.
6. Remove the pickles from the oil and drain on paper towels. Eat plain or serve with ketchup or ranch dressing.

# Pan-seared Pork Chops with Applesauce

**Makes:** 4 servings
**Prep:** 5 mins
**Cook:** 15 mins

**Ingredients**

2 tablespoons canola oil
1 teaspoon Italian seasoning
½ teaspoon garlic powder
4 boneless pork chops
½ cup onions, diced
¾ cup chunky **applesauce**
2 tablespoons parsley, chopped
¼ cup water
salt and pepper, to taste

1. Combine the oil, Italian seasoning, and garlic powder in a bowl to make a marinade. Season to taste with salt and pepper.
2. Coat the pork chops in the marinade. Let pork chops marinate in the refrigerator for at least 1 hour.
3. Place a nonstick pan on medium-high heat. When the pan is hot, add the pork chops.
4. Cook the pork chops until they're cooked through, about 4 minutes on each side. Remove from pan and set aside.
5. In the same pan, add the onions and cook for another 5 minutes, stirring often.
6. Stir in the applesauce, parsley, and ¼ cup of water, and cook for another minute.
7. Season with more salt and pepper, then spoon the applesauce over the pork chops.

# Let's Pick Apples!

Nothing says fall like apple picking! Here are some tips to make your next apple picking adventure a good one.

- If you want apples that are ready to eat, focus your search on the outside of the apple tree because apples on the outer branches ripen first.
- To pick an apple correctly, pull the apple up off the branch and give it a twist to remove.
- Put your picked apples in your bag or basket gently. Bruises will cause your apples to rot faster.

# Sweet Potato Fries

**Serves:** 4
**Prep:** 10 mins
**Cook:** 15–20 mins

**Ingredients**

1 tablespoon oil
4 small **sweet potatoes** (about 1½ pounds)
½ teaspoon salt
½ teaspoon ground cumin
¼ teaspoon cayenne pepper

1. Preheat the oven to 450°F. Brush a large baking sheet with a little of the oil.
2. Peel the sweet potatoes and slice into ¼-inch-thick spears about 3 inches long. Spread the sweet potatoes on the prepared baking sheet, pour over the remaining oil, and mix to coat.
3. In a small bowl, combine the salt, cumin, and cayenne pepper. Sprinkle the spice mixture evenly over the sweet potatoes and then mix again.
4. Spread the sweet potatoes out into a single layer and bake in the preheated oven for 15–20 minutes or until cooked through and lightly colored.

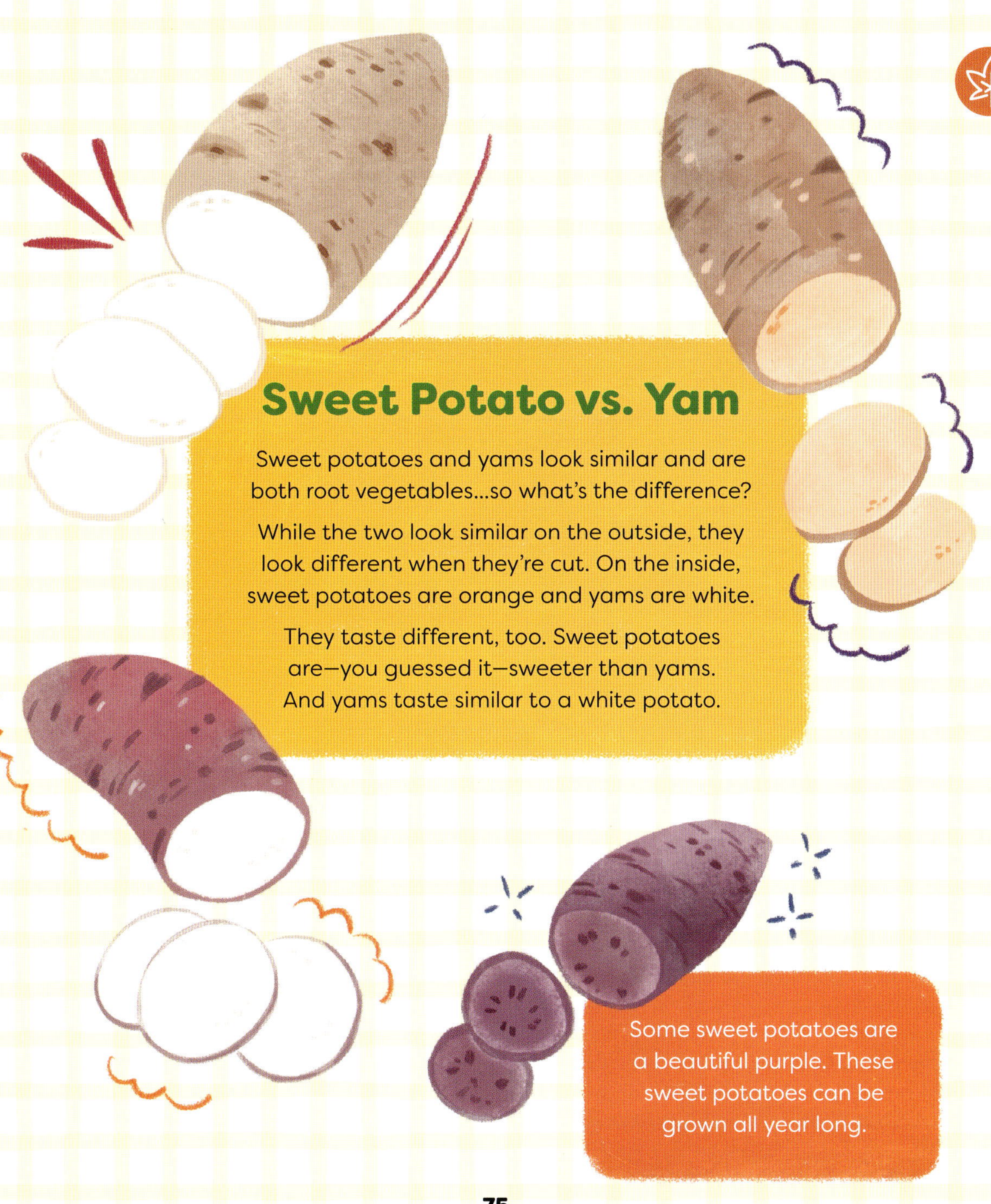

## Sweet Potato vs. Yam

Sweet potatoes and yams look similar and are both root vegetables...so what's the difference?

While the two look similar on the outside, they look different when they're cut. On the inside, sweet potatoes are orange and yams are white.

They taste different, too. Sweet potatoes are—you guessed it—sweeter than yams. And yams taste similar to a white potato.

Some sweet potatoes are a beautiful purple. These sweet potatoes can be grown all year long.

# Sweet Potato Ravioli with Brown Butter Sage Sauce

**Makes:** 4 servings
**Prep:** 15 mins
**Cook:** 60 mins

**Ingredients**

nonstick cooking spray
2 medium **sweet potatoes**, halved lengthwise
2 tablespoons ricotta cheese
1 tablespoon brown sugar
6 tablespoons unsalted butter
2 pounds homemade pasta or 1 package premade sheets of pasta dough cut into 3x3-inch squares
6 fresh sage leaves, thinly sliced
2 tablespoons pecans, chopped
2 tablespoons Pecorino Romano cheese, grated
salt and pepper, to taste

1. Preheat the oven to 400°F.
2. Spray a baking sheet with nonstick cooking spray.
3. Put the sweet potatoes cut-side down on the baking sheet. Roast until tender, about 35–40 minutes. Check with a fork to see if they're done.
4. When cooked, allow some time for them to cool, then scoop the insides out from the skin. Put in a bowl.
5. Add ricotta, brown sugar, and 1 tablespoon of butter to the sweet potatoes. Mix together with a fork. Season with salt and pepper.
6. Put a square of pasta dough on a flat surface. Add about 2 teaspoons of filling in the middle of the square.

7. Use your fingertip to brush a small amount of water along the edges of the square.
8. Add a second square over the filling and press down on the edges with a fork to seal them. Do this with all the dough squares and rest of the filling.
9. Fill a large pot with salted water and bring to a boil over high heat.
10. Add the ravioli to the pot and cook until they float to the top, about 2 minutes. Drain and set aside. Make sure cooked ravioli aren't stacked together before the sauce is added—they'll stick together.
11. To make the sauce, heat the rest of the butter in a pan until it's melted. Add the sage leaves and chopped pecans.
12. Cook for about 3–5 minutes. The butter should turn a medium brown color.
13. Pour the sauce over the ravioli. Serve with grated cheese.

## Homemade Pasta

**Makes:** 4 servings
**Prep:** 5 mins
**Rest:** 30 mins

**Ingredients**

4 cups all-purpose or semolina flour
4 eggs

1. Put 4 cups of all-purpose or semolina flour on a clean working surface. Make a well in the center.
2. Crack 4 eggs into the well.
3. Gently beat the eggs together with a fork, gathering and mixing flour into the egg mixture as you go until all flour is combined. (Tip: If your dough is dry, you can add a teaspoon of water at a time until it sticks together.)
4. When the dough forms a ball, cover in plastic wrap and let it rest for at least 30 minutes.
5. After the dough has rested, cut the ball into 4 equal sections.
6. Roll out each section using a floured rolling pin until you have one big, thin sheet. Cut the sheets into squares about 3x3 inches to make ravioli, or strips to make long noodles.

# How to Prep Squash for Cooking

Squash is a nutritious vegetable! It can be a little hard to work with because of its thick skin, hard flesh, and wonky shape. Here are some tips to help:

1. Always wash and dry the squash before cutting.
2. With a grown-up's help, use a peeler or a sharp knife to remove the skin from the squash.
3. Once the squash is peeled, you can cut it. First, cut off both ends of the squash, then cut it in half down the middle. If the squash is very firm, place the knife on the squash, cover it with a kitchen towel, and carefully hit the back of the knife with something heavy to help split it open.
4. Cut the squash in half again, or in quarters. Then, using a spoon, scoop out the seeds.
5. Now you can dice, chop, or slice the squash and cook with it!

# Pasta in Butternut Squash Sauce

**Makes:** 8 servings
**Prep:** 10 mins
**Cook:** 60 mins

**Ingredients**

3 tablespoons olive oil
2 pounds **butternut squash**, seeded, peeled, and cubed
1 medium yellow onion, peeled and quartered
4–5 garlic cloves, peel on
1 cup vegetable broth
1 (15-ounce) can white beans, rinsed and drained
¼ teaspoon nutmeg
4 cups cooked pasta
plain yogurt, to stir in, or Parmesan cheese, grated

1. Preheat the oven to 400°F.
2. Line a baking sheet with parchment paper.
3. In a bowl, toss oil over vegetables until they're well coated.
4. Place them on the baking sheet, then roast until squash is tender, about 30–45 minutes. Check by piercing the squash with a fork.
5. Let the vegetables cool, then squeeze the garlic out of its peel into a food processor. Add the rest of the vegetables along with the broth, beans, and nutmeg. Blend until smooth.
6. Pour the sauce into a pan over medium-low heat. Heat until warmed through.
7. Add cooked pasta to the sauce and mix. Stir in yogurt or cheese to serve.

# Kale Pesto Spaghetti

**Makes:** 4 servings
**Prep:** 20 mins
**Cook:** 20 mins

**Ingredients**

8 ounces **kale**
3 tablespoons pine nuts
1 pound spaghetti
1 large garlic clove
½ cup olive oil
zest of 1 lemon, plus juice from one half
1 ounce Parmesan cheese, grated, plus extra to serve
1½ cups canned cannellini beans
2 tablespoons chia seeds, to garnish
¾ teaspoon salt, plus more to taste

1. Bring a large saucepan of salted water to a boil, and fill a medium-sized bowl with ice water.
2. Trim the stems and center parts from the kale, then place the leaves in the boiling water for 45 seconds.
3. Using a slotted spoon, transfer the kale to the ice water.
4. Drain the kale, place it on a clean towel, and squeeze to remove any water.
5. Heat a large frying pan over medium heat, place a layer of parchment paper on the base, and scatter the pine nuts on top. Gently toast until the nuts turn golden. Set aside.
6. Bring the saucepan of salted water back to a boil and add the pasta. Cook for 8–10 minutes until tender.

3

5

7

7. While the pasta is cooking, combine the kale, pine nuts, garlic, and ¾ teaspoon of salt in a food processor.
8. Zest the lemon into the processor, then halve the lemon and squeeze in the juice of one half. Pulse until smooth. Drizzle in the oil until it is fully incorporated. Add the cheese and pulse to mix.
9. Drain and rinse the beans, then add to the pasta.
10. Drain the pasta, but save some of the cooking water. Toss the pasta and beans with the pesto. Add a little of the pasta water, if needed, to coat the pasta nicely.
11. Serve with cheese and a sprinkling of chia seeds.

## Kale Knowledge

Kale is part of the same family as broccoli, brussels sprouts, and cabbage. It's called the cruciferous family.

Kale is packed full of calcium, potassium, iron, and vitamins A, C, and K. That's a lot of nutrients for a leaf!

# Bite-size Broccoli Facts

Broccoli gets its name from the Italian word "broccolo," which means "the flowering top of a cabbage."

There's no good machine for harvesting broccoli, so each broccoli head must be picked by hand when it's done growing.

# Roasted Broccoli
## with Pine Nuts & Parmesan

**Makes:** 4 servings
**Prep:** 20 mins
**Bake:** 25 mins

**Ingredients**

1½ heads of **broccoli**
1 teaspoon olive oil
1 teaspoon sea salt
¼ teaspoon ground black pepper
¼ cup toasted pine nuts
zest of ½ lemon
1 ounce Parmesan cheese shavings
4 lemon wedges, to garnish

1. Preheat the oven to 450°F.
2. Cut off the broccoli crowns where they meet the stalk.
3. Remove the outer peel from the stalks. Slice the stalks crosswise into 3¼-inch pieces, then quarter each slice lengthwise. Cut the crown into 1½-inch-wide wedges.
4. Put the broccoli wedges and stalks into a bowl. Sprinkle with the oil, salt, and pepper, gently tossing to coat.
5. Spread out the broccoli in a large roasting pan. Cover tightly with aluminum foil and roast on the bottom rack of the oven for 10 minutes.
6. Remove the foil, then roast for an additional 5–8 minutes until just starting to brown. Turn the stalks and wedges over, and roast for an additional 3–5 minutes until tender.
7. Transfer to a shallow serving dish, along with any cooking juices.
8. Sprinkle with the pine nuts and lemon zest, tossing to mix.
9. Sprinkle the cheese shavings over the top. Garnish with lemon wedges.

# Fruit and Vegetable Stamp Art

Fruits and vegetables aren't just for eating—you can use them to make art, too!

**What You'll Need**

- produce of your choice, sliced in half—some good options are celery hearts, bell peppers, potatoes, cucumbers, apples, mushrooms, grapes, oranges, and corn
- nontoxic, washable paint
- white paper
- paper plates

1. Pour paint onto individual paper plates.
2. Dip a piece of produce into the paint, cut-side down.
3. Stamp the piece of produce on the white paper, cut-side down.
4. Continue doing this with various fruits and vegetables, making different patterns on your paper.
5. When you're done, let your artwork fully dry before displaying your finished piece.

SNACKS

# Chewy Apricot & Almond Energy Bars

**Makes:** 15
**Prep:** 25 mins, plus cooling
**Bake:** 30 mins

**Ingredients**

½ cup coconut oil
⅓ cup brown sugar
4 tablespoons nut butter
1 apple, cored and grated
⅔ cup oats
3 tablespoons all-purpose flour
¼ cup raw almonds, roughly chopped
3 tablespoons sunflower seeds
¾ cup dried **apricots**, diced

1. Preheat the oven to 350°F.
2. Line an 8-inch shallow square pan with parchment paper.
3. Heat the oil and sugar in a medium-size saucepan over low heat until the oil has melted and the sugar is dissolved.
4. Remove from the heat, then stir in the nut butter until melted.
5. Add the apple, oats, flour, almonds, and sunflower seeds, and mix together well.
6. Spoon two-thirds of the mixture into the prepared dish and press down firmly.

**7.** Sprinkle over the apricots and press firmly into the base layer, then dot the remaining oat mixture over the top in a thin layer so some of the apricots are still visible.

**8.** Bake for about 25 minutes until the top is golden brown.

**9.** Remove from the oven and leave to cool completely. Then cut into 15 small rectangles.

**10.** Lift the bars out of the dish, using the paper. Store in a plastic container in the refrigerator for up to 3 days.

Apricot means "precious" in Latin.

# Carrots Are Not Just for Bunnies

You can eat all parts of a carrot. Its seeds can be used as flavoring, the flowers can be added to salads, and the leaves can be made into sauces or sautéed and eaten by themselves!

Have you ever seen a purple carrot? They exist! Carrots come in orange, white, yellow, and purple.

# Carrot Cake Muffins

**Makes:** 10
**Prep:** 20–25 mins
**Bake:** 25 mins

**Ingredients**

3 ¾ cups all-purpose flour
1 teaspoon baking soda
1 teaspoon baking powder
½ teaspoon salt
1 teaspoon ground cinnamon
¼ teaspoon ground ginger
2 tablespoons canola oil
2 eggs
3 tablespoons granulated sugar
2 teaspoons vanilla extract
½ cup applesauce
⅓ cup milk
7–8 **carrots** (1 pound)
½ cup raisins
½ cup chopped walnuts
¾ cup coconut flakes

1. Preheat the oven to 350°F.
2. Line 10 cups in a 12-cup muffin pan with paper liners.
3. Sift together the flour, baking soda, baking powder, salt, cinnamon, and ginger into a bowl.
4. Beat together the oil, eggs, sugar, and vanilla extract in a bowl until creamy, then stir in the applesauce and milk.
5. Peel and shred the carrots, then add to the liquid ingredients with the raisins, walnuts, and half the coconut. Add the flour mixture, stirring until just combined.
6. Divide the batter among the paper liners. Bake for 25 minutes until a toothpick inserted into the center of a muffin comes out clean.
7. Let cool in the pan, then transfer to a wire rack and let cool completely. Garnish with the remaining coconut.

# Fruit Cocktail Pops

**Makes:** 8
**Prep:** 35 mins, plus 6+ hrs of cooling & freezing
**Cook:** 6–8 mins

### Ingredients

1 cup strawberries, hulled
2 small ripe **peaches**, peeled, stoned, and roughly chopped, or 9 ounces canned peaches, drained
4 large kiwis, peeled and roughly chopped

### Sugar Syrup

2 tablespoons granulated sugar
5 tablespoons water

### You Will Also Need

8 (4-ounce) ice pop molds
8 ice pop sticks

1. To make the sugar syrup, put the sugar and water into a small saucepan over low heat and stir until the sugar has dissolved. Raise the heat, bring to a boil, then lower the heat again and simmer for 3–4 minutes. Remove from heat and leave to cool completely before using.
2. Put the strawberries in a blender and pulse until pureed. Stir in 2 tablespoons of the sugar syrup.
3. Pour the mixture into the ice pop molds. Freeze for 2 hours or until firm.
4. Put the peaches in the blender and pulse until pureed. Stir in half the remaining sugar syrup.
5. Pour the peach mixture over the frozen strawberry mixture. Insert the ice pop sticks and freeze for 2 hours or until firm.

6. Put the kiwis in the blender and pulse until pureed. Stir in the remaining sugar syrup.
7. Pour the kiwi mixture over the frozen peach mixture and freeze for 2 hours or until firm.
8. To remove the ice pops, dip the molds in warm water for a few seconds and gently pull the pops out while holding the sticks.

## Why Are Peaches Fuzzy?

Peaches have skin like many other fruits. But their skin is a little different—it's fuzzy!

Peach skin has tiny little hairs all over it. Those fuzzy little hairs keep the inside of the fruit, which is delicate, safe from bugs and too much water getting in.

A peach is a stone fruit, which means there is a hard pit at its center. When a recipe asks you to "stone" a fruit, it means you should remove the center stone before chopping the fruit.

## Why Are Bees Important?

- Bees are our planet's most important pollinators. A pollinator helps carry pollen between the female and male parts of a plant. This allows those plants to grow seeds and fruit. When bees pollinate the plants around us, they're helping make the food we—and animals—eat to grow big and strong!
- In the United States alone, bees help pollinate more than 100 types of crops.
- Honeybees create honey, but not every type of bee makes honey. Other bees, like bumblebees, mason bees, and mining bees, also do important pollinating work.

# Honey & Blueberry Bars

**Makes:** 12 bars
**Prep:** 15 mins
**Bake:** 30 mins, plus cooling

**Ingredients**

oil, for greasing
⅔ cup all-purpose flour
½ teaspoon baking powder
½ cup quinoa flakes
3 ⅔ cups puffed rice
½ cup slivered almonds
1 ½ cups blueberries
8 tablespoons butter
⅓ cup plus 1 tablespoon **honey**
1 egg, beaten

1. Preheat the oven to 350°F.
2. Brush an 11x7-inch baking pan with oil and line with parchment paper.
3. Sift together the flour and baking powder, then mix with the quinoa flakes, puffed rice, almonds, and blueberries in a bowl.
4. Heat the butter and honey in a saucepan over low heat until melted.
5. Pour the melted mixture over the dry ingredients. Add the egg, and stir well.
6. Spoon the batter into the pan. Make an even layer using a spatula.
7. Bake for 25–30 minutes until golden brown and firm. Let cool in the pan for 15 minutes, then cut into 12 bars and transfer to a wire rack to cool completely.

# Roasted Red Bell Pepper Bruschetta

**Makes:** 16 servings
**Prep:** 15 mins
**Bake:** 8 mins

**Ingredients**

16 slices French bread, sliced diagonally, ½ inch thick
¼ cup olive oil
8–10 large cloves garlic, cut in half
1 (7-ounce) jar roasted **red bell peppers**, drained
2 tablespoons Italian parsley, chopped
2 tablespoons Parmesan cheese, shredded
¼ teaspoon salt
¼ teaspoon pepper

1. Heat the oven to 375°F.
2. Put the pieces of bread on an ungreased baking sheet.
3. Drizzle olive oil on each slice of bread.
4. Bake the slices until they're golden brown, usually about 4 minutes on each side.
5. Rub the cut sides of the garlic cloves over the tops of the bread slices. Throw away garlic when done.
6. Cut the peppers into ½-inch strips.
7 In a bowl, mix together the peppers, parsley, cheese, salt, and pepper.
8. Spoon the pepper mixture on each slice of bread.

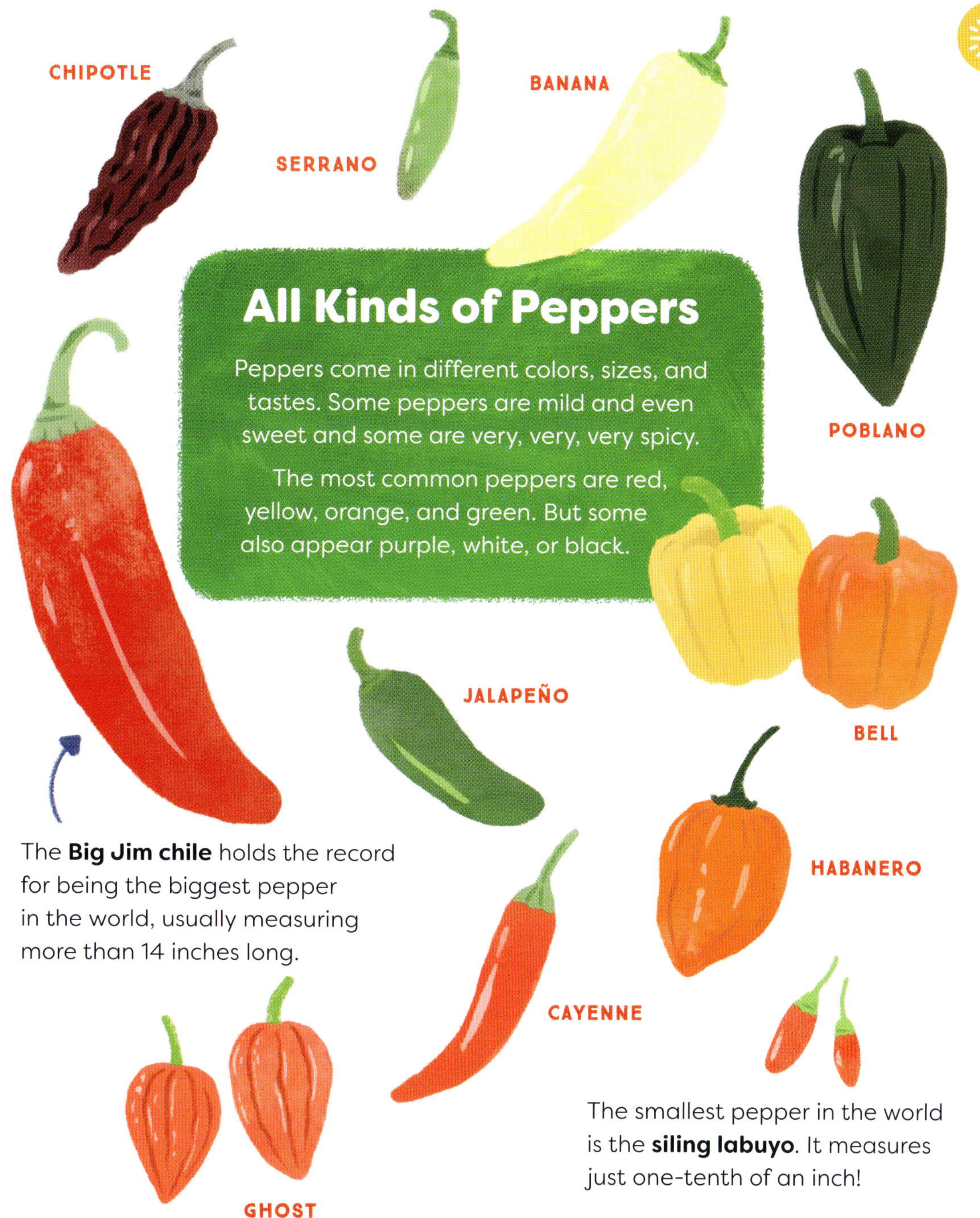


## All Kinds of Peppers

Peppers come in different colors, sizes, and tastes. Some peppers are mild and even sweet and some are very, very, very spicy.

The most common peppers are red, yellow, orange, and green. But some also appear purple, white, or black.

The **Big Jim chile** holds the record for being the biggest pepper in the world, usually measuring more than 14 inches long.

The smallest pepper in the world is the **siling labuyo**. It measures just one-tenth of an inch!

# Air Fryer Tempura Green Beans with Spicy Ranch Dipping Sauce

**Makes** 4 servings
**Prep:** 15 mins
**Cook:** 10 mins

**Ingredients**

nonstick cooking spray
1 pound fresh **green beans**, washed and trimmed
¾ cup bread crumbs
¼ cup Parmesan cheese, grated
¼ teaspoon garlic powder
¼ teaspoon onion powder
¼ teaspoon paprika
½ teaspoon ground black pepper
½ cup all-purpose flour
2 eggs

The color of this type of beans is in the name: green. But some can be purple, yellow, or have spots!

1. In a bowl, combine the bread crumbs, Parmesan, garlic powder, onion powder, paprika, and pepper.
2. In another bowl, whisk eggs until light and fluffy.
3. Roll green beans in flour, then dip them in the egg mixture.
4. Finally, coat them in the bread crumbs.
5. Heat the air fryer to 390°F. Spray the basket with nonstick cooking spray.
6. Place the green beans in the basket in a single layer and cook for 5 minutes. Shake the basket to toss and cook the green beans for another 2–3 minutes.

**Spicy Ranch Dipping Sauce**

1 cup ranch dressing
2 teaspoons sriracha sauce

To make the dipping sauce, mix together the ranch dressing and sriracha sauce in a small bowl.

## Grow, Grow, Grow, Green Beans!

There are two types of green beans: pole beans and bush beans. Pole beans grow like vines and need a structure to support them. Bush beans grow on the ground and don't need any structure to help them.

# Homemade Spiced Nut Butter

**Makes:** 1 cup
**Prep:** 15 mins

**Ingredients**

1 cup unsalted **peanuts or nuts** (almonds, hazelnuts, cashews, walnuts, etc.)
1 teaspoon salt
1 teaspoon paprika
1½ teaspoons oil

1. Place the nuts and salt in a small food processor. Pulse until the nuts progress from a crumble to a paste and then to a thick, creamy consistency.
2. Add the paprika and blend for another 30 seconds.
3. Drizzle in the oil and blend again.
4. Store the spiced nut butter in a lidded jar or airtight plastic container in the refrigerator for up to 5 days.

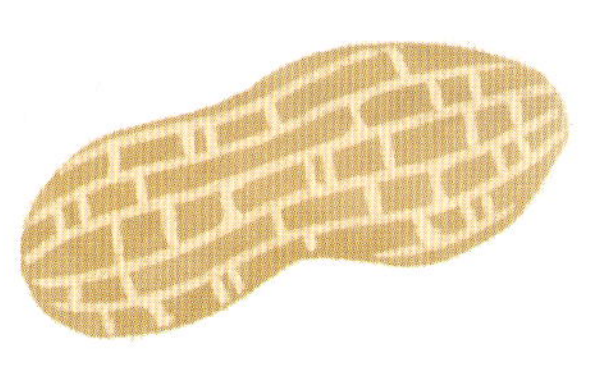

## Nuts About...Nuts!

- Did you know a peanut isn't actually a nut? It's a legume! A legume is part of the same family as beans, lentils, and peas.
- Peanuts grow in the ground, whereas nuts like almonds, walnuts, and hazelnuts grow on trees.
- It's very easy to substitute peanut butter with a different nut butter. Nut butters can be made from different kinds of nuts, like almonds, hazelnuts, and pistachios.

## Jam, Jelly, or Preserve?

Do you know how to tell these three apart?

Jam is made by boiling mashed fruit and sugar together until it combines into a thick consistency.

Jelly is made by combining fruit juice with gelatin or pectin. It is usually a jiggly consistency.

Preserves are jams made with whole or large pieces of fruit.

# Easy Raspberry Jam

**Makes:** 1 (12-ounces) jar
**Prep:** 10 mins
**Cook:** 20 mins

**Ingredients**

1 pound fresh or frozen raspberries
¼ cup water
1 cup granulated sugar
large pinch salt
1 tablespoon lemon juice

1. Combine all ingredients in a large saucepan over medium heat.
2. Mash the ingredients together using a fork.
3. Bring the mixture to a boil and cook, stirring occassionally, for about 20 minutes. Remove from heat. Remember: the jam will thicken as it cools.
4. Once it's cooled completely, pour into an airtight jar. It will last for up to 3 weeks in the refrigerator.

## What Is a Root Vegetable?

A root vegetable is the part of a plant that grows underground and can be eaten. They taste good because their job is to make energy in the form of sugar to send up to the plant's flowers. Some root vegetables are potatoes, carrots, turnips, radishes, and onions.

TURNIP
SWEET POTATO
BEET
CARROT

# Root Vegetable Chips
## with Herby Yogurt Dip

**Makes:** 4 servings
**Prep:** 30–35 mins
**Bake:** 12–16 mins, plus cooling

### Ingredients

2 ¼ pounds mixed **root vegetables**, such as carrots, sweet potatoes, parsnips, or beets
4 tablespoons olive oil
sea salt and pepper, to taste

1. Preheat the oven to 400°F. Peel the root vegetables.
2. Slice the root vegetables very thinly. Using a mandolin—with a grown-up's help—will make this easy to do.
3. Put the vegetables in a large bowl. Add the olive oil, salt, and pepper. Toss until all the vegetables are coated.
4. Arrange the vegetables over three baking sheets in a single layer.
5. Bake for 8–10 minutes, then check. The slices in the corners of the trays will cook more quickly, so transfer any that are crisp and golden to a wire rack. Cook the rest for 2–3 minutes more, then transfer any more cooked slices to the wire rack. Repeat until all the vegetables are crisp.
6. Allow to cool, then arrange the chips in a bowl and spoon the dip into a smaller bowl to serve.

### Herby Yogurt Dip

7 ounces plain Greek yogurt
2 garlic cloves, minced
4 tablespoons fresh herbs, such as parsley, chives, basil, or oregano, minced
salt and pepper, to taste

Mix the yogurt, garlic, and herbs in a small bowl, then season with salt and pepper. Cover and chill in the refrigerator until ready to eat.

# Pink Energy Bars

**Makes:** 10 bars
**Prep:** 6 mins, plus chilling

**Ingredients**

½ cup oats
½ cup ground almonds (almond meal)
2 tablespoons creamy peanut butter
1 small roasted **beet**, any variety
1 tablespoon maple syrup

1. Put the oats in a food processor and process until broken down.
2. Add the remaining ingredients and process again until the mixture is combined.
3. Press the dough into a 5-inch square pan and smooth into an even layer. Chill in the refrigerator for 1 hour, then cut into bars.

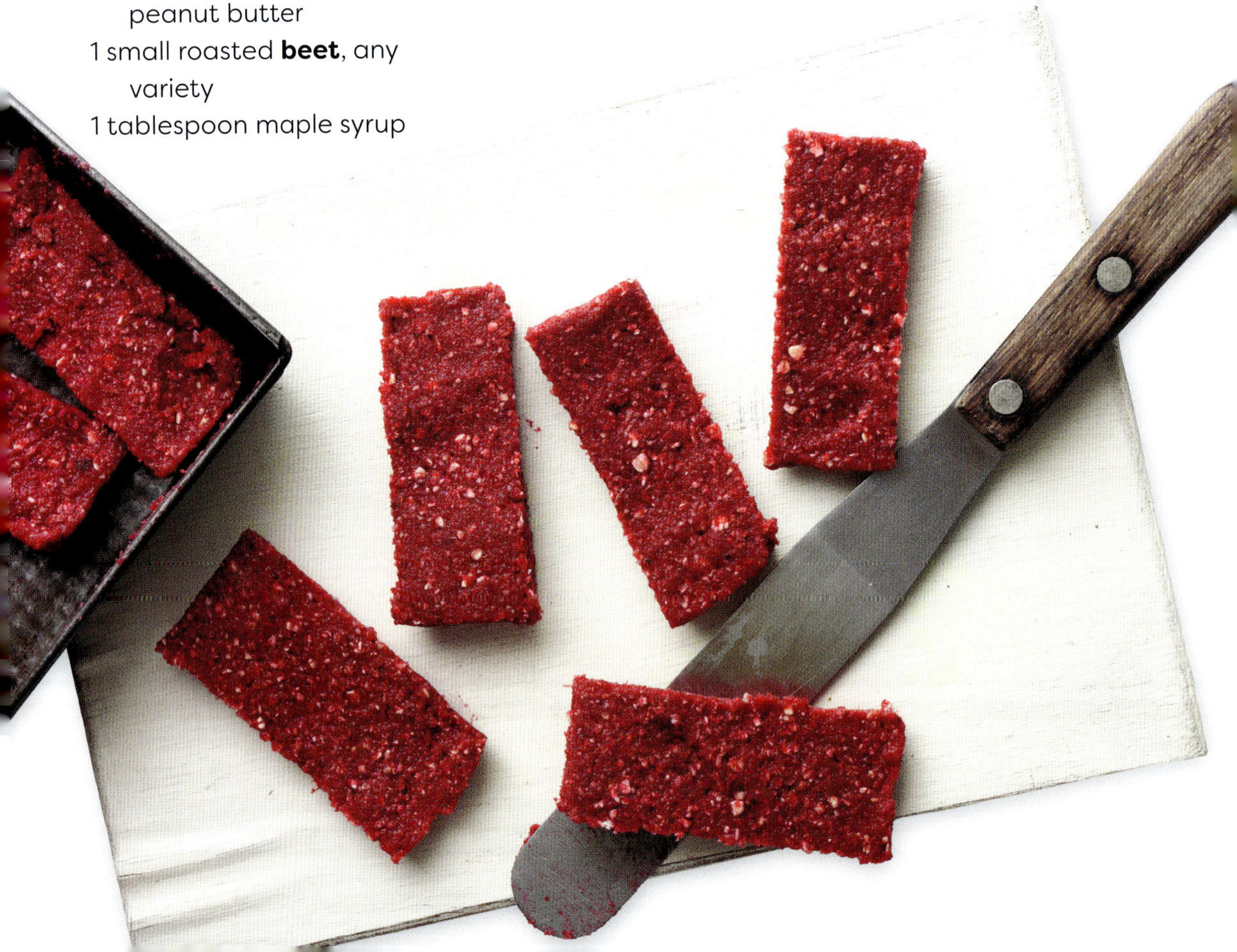

CYLINDRA

# How to Roast Beets

AVALANCHE

1. Preheat the oven to 400°F.
2. Cut the tops off the beets and scrub them well. Make sure to use gloves when handling beets as they can stain your skin.
3. Put beets in a bowl and drizzle generously with olive oil, then season with salt and pepper.
4. Wrap the beets in aluminum foil and place on a baking sheet. Roast for 35–60 minutes or until the beets are tender when testing with a fork.
5. Remove the beets from the oven, take off the foil, and set aside to cool. Once cooled, use a dry paper towel to remove the skins before using. Wear gloves when doing this, too!

DETROIT DARK RED

WHITE DETROIT

GOLDEN

EARLY WONDER

# Sweet Sugar

Sugar comes from different sources around the world, and can be used in cooking and baking to make delicious treats.

Cane sugar is sugar made from the sugarcane plant.

Agave is a plant that's mostly found growing in Mexico. Agave syrup is made when the core of the plant is heated, juiced, filtered, and evaporated until a sweet syrup is created.

Corn syrup is a sweet syrup made when cornstarch is broken down.

Honey starts as nectar that bees collect from flowers. The nectar is stored inside the honeycomb of a beehive, where bees work hard to create liquid honey.

Beet sugar is made by taking the juice of sugar beets, heating it to make a syrup, then hardening it to create granulated beet sugar.

Maple syrup is made from concentrated sap collected from the sugar maple tree.

SWEET THINGS

# Strawberry Nice Cream

**Makes:** 6 servings
**Prep:** 30 mins, plus freezing

**Ingredients**

1 pound **strawberries**, hulled and halved
1½ cup canned full-fat coconut milk
⅓ cup honey
crushed hazelnuts, to serve, if desired

1. Puree the strawberries in a food processor, then press through a sieve over a mixing bowl to remove the seeds.
2. Add the coconut milk and honey to the strawberry puree and whisk together.
3. Pour the mixture into a large roasting dish, cover the top of the dish with plastic wrap, then freeze for about 2 hours until just set.
4. Scoop back into the food processor and blitz again until smooth, to break down the ice crystals.

5. Pour into a plastic container lined with parchment paper. Fold the paper over the ice cream and return to the freezer for 3–4 hours until firm enough to scoop.
6. When ready to serve, thaw at room temperature to soften slightly, then scoop into individual dishes and top with crushed hazelnuts if desired.

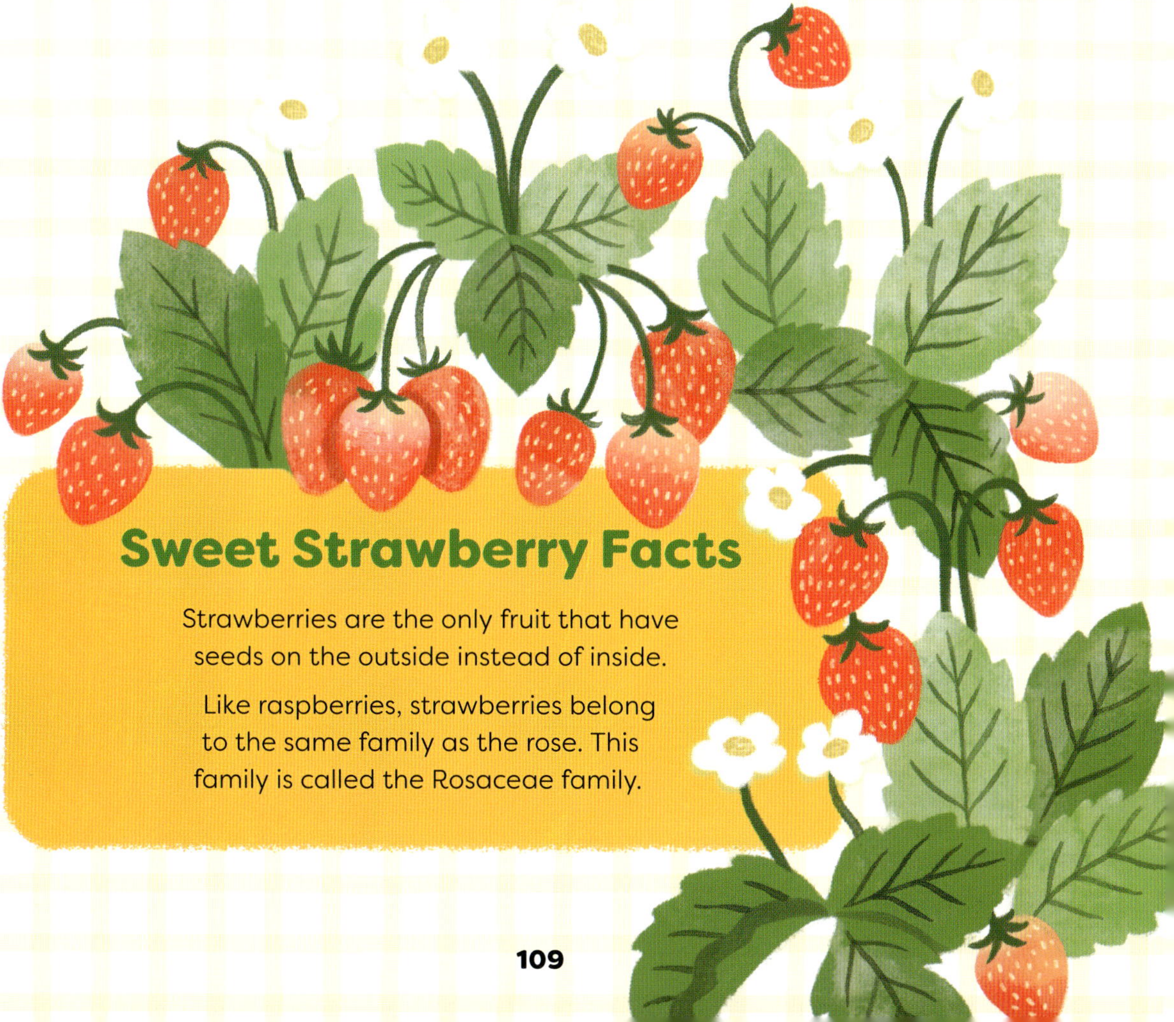

## Sweet Strawberry Facts

Strawberries are the only fruit that have seeds on the outside instead of inside.

Like raspberries, strawberries belong to the same family as the rose. This family is called the Rosaceae family.

# Cherry Hand Pies

**Makes:** 8
**Prep:** 15 mins
**Bake:** 20 mins, plus cooling

**Ingredients**

pie crust for 9-inch double-crust pie
1 large egg
1 tablespoon water
2 cups **cherry** pie filling
turbinado sugar

1. Preheat the oven to 400°F.
2. Line a baking sheet with parchment paper.
3. On a floured work surface, roll the pie dough into a 12x20-inch rectangle.
4. Cut the dough into 16 rectangles. Each should be about 5x6 inches. (Optional: Use a heart-shaped cookie cutter to cut out 16 pieces.)
5. Put 2 tablespoons of cherry filling in the middle of each rectangle or heart-shaped piece of dough.

6. Make an egg wash by whisking the egg and water together.
7. Use a pastry brush to brush a small amount of egg wash along the edges of the dough. Then place another rectangle or heart-shaped piece of dough on top of the filling. (Optional: Use a small heart-shaped cookie cutter to cut a small heart from the center of the dough before placing on top of the filling.) Use a fork to seal edges.
8. Put the pies on the baking sheet.
9. If you don't cut a small heart into the top of the pie, use a knife to cut three small slits in the top of each pie.
10. Brush the tops of each pie with more egg wash, then sprinkle the sugar on top.
11. Bake for about 20 minutes or until the pie crust is golden brown and the filling has started to bubble.
12. Leave to cool on the baking sheet for a few minutes before transfering to a wire rack to cool completely.

BING

BLACK

MONTMORENCY

## Cherry-picked Facts

On average, a cherry tree will grow 7,000 cherries every year!

There are two types of cherries: sweet and tart. Sweet cherries are better for eating and tart cherries are best for baking because they hold their shape better in baked goods.

RAINIER

QUEEN ANNE

TULARE

MORELLO

WATERMELON

MUSKMELON

## Mighty Melons

Melons are very nutritious. All melons have lots of vitamin A and C, and most have minerals like iron, calcium, potassium, and magnesium.

It's believed that watermelon was first grown in Africa more than 4,000 years ago!

CUCUMBER

HONEYDEW

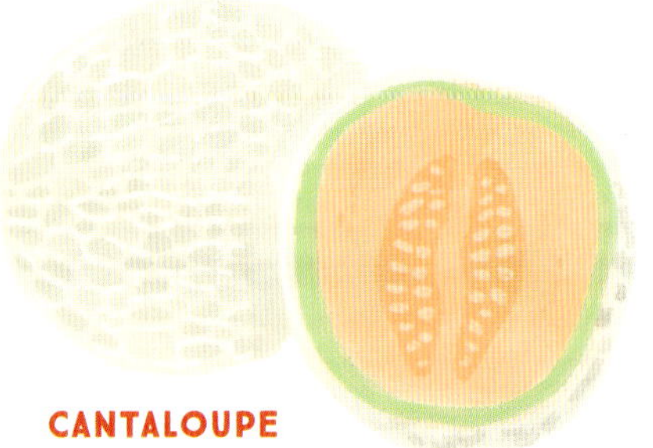

CANTALOUPE

A **cucamelon** is a melon from Mexico and Central America. It's the size of a grape, looks like a watermelon, and tastes like a cucumber.

# Watermelon Roll-ups

**Makes:** 18 servings
**Prep:** 15 mins
**Bake:** 3–4 hrs

**Ingredients**

nonstick cooking spray
8 cups **watermelon**, cubed
½ cup granulated sugar
juice of 1 lime

1. Preheat the oven to 170°F.
2. Place a piece of parchment paper on a rimmed baking sheet and lightly cover with the cooking spray.
3. Put the watermelon cubes in a blender and blend until smooth.
4. Using a fine mesh strainer, drain the liquid from the puree. There should be about 2 cups of watermelon solids left.
5. In a bowl, whisk together pureed watermelon mixture, sugar, and lime juice.
6. Pour the mixture on the baking sheet. Use a spatula to create an even layer.
7. Bake for about 3–4 hours until the mixture is dried and not sticky.
8. Use scissors to cut the fruit leather into strips, then roll them up. Store in an airtight container.

# Whipped Cream Marshmallow Fruit Salad

**Makes:** 6 servings
**Prep:** 5 mins

**Ingredients**

1 (15-ounce) can mandarin oranges, drained
1 (20-ounce) can pineapple tidbits, drained
6 ounces (½ jar) maraschino cherries, drained and chopped, reserve 6 for serving
1 cup miniature marshmallows
2 cups **whipped cream**
sprinkles, to garnish, optional

1. In a large bowl, gently mix together the oranges, pineapple, cherries, and marshmallows.
2. Fold in the whipped cream until everything is combined.
3. Divide the salad into bowls and garnish with a maraschino cherry and sprinkles.

# How to Make Whipped Cream

You can buy whipped cream in the store, but you can make it yourself and it's even more delicious.

**Makes:** 2 cups
**Prep:** 5 mins, plus chilling

**Ingredients**

¼ cup cold heavy whipping cream
½ cup confectioners' sugar
½ teaspoon vanilla extract

1. If using a stand mixer, place that bowl in the refrigerator to chill for at least 15–30 minutes. If using a mixing bowl, use a glass or metal one so it can easily get cold in the refrigerator.
2. Once the bowl is chilled, add the heavy whipping cream, confectioners' sugar, and vanilla.
3. Whisk the ingredients together until the mixture starts to thicken. Stop to scrape the sides of the bowl if necessary.
4. Once peaks have started to form, remove from the bowl and serve or store in an airtight container and keep refrigerated until use.

WHIPPING CREAM

Cream comes from cows, just like milk! Cream has more fat than milk, which is how it can be turned into fluffy, tasty whipped cream!

# Types of Apples

You've probably seen lots of types of apples at the grocery store, but there are even more around the world—7,500 to be exact! And 2,500 of those types are grown in the United States.

**MOST TART**

- GRANNY SMITH
- MCINTOSH
- PINK LADY
- GOLDEN DELICIOUS
- BRAEBURN
- RED DELICIOUS
- HONEYCRISP
- GALA
- JONAGOLD
- FUJI

**SWEETEST**

# Apple Crumble

**Makes:** 6 servings
**Prep:** 25 mins
**Bake:** 40–45 mins

**Ingredients**

1 pound baking **apples**, like Granny Smith or Pink Lady, peeled, cored, and chopped into chunks
¼ teaspoon ground cloves
¼ teaspoon ground cinnamon
1 teaspoon ground ginger
3 tablespoons brown sugar

**Topping**

1 cup oats
½ teaspoon ground cinnamon
3 tablespoons honey
3 tablespoons coconut oil, room temperature
3½ tablespoons macadamia nuts, roughly chopped
2 tablespoons brown sugar

1. Preheat the oven to 350°F.
2. Place the apple chunks in a large saucepan. Add 2 tablespoons of cold water, the cloves, cinnamon, ginger, and brown sugar, and place over medium heat.
3. Cook for about 15 minutes, stirring regularly, until the apples begin to soften.
4. Transfer the apples to a 12-inch pie pan.
5. To make the topping, place the oats in a medium-size bowl. Stir in the cinnamon, honey, coconut oil, macadamia nuts, and brown sugar, and mix well.
6. Sprinkle the mixture over the stewed apples and bake for 25–30 minutes until golden. Remove from the oven and leave to cool for a few minutes before serving.

# Mini Pumpkin Pies

**Makes:** 12
**Prep:** 5 mins
**Bake:** 20 mins

**Ingredients**

12 ready-made tart shells
1 cup canned **pumpkin** puree or unsweetened pie filling
⅓ cup brown sugar
2 eggs, lightly beaten
2 tablespoons maple syrup
½ cup evaporated milk
1 teaspoon ground cinnamon
½ teaspoon ground ginger
¼ teaspoon ground cloves
whipped cream, to serve
nutmeg, grated, to serve

1. Preheat the oven to 375°F.
2. Place the tart shells on a large baking sheet. Put the pumpkin puree and sugar into a large bowl and beat together with a wooden spoon.
3. Add the eggs, maple syrup, evaporated milk, and spices, and whisk until combined.
4. Carefully pour the mixture evenly into the tart shells.
5. Bake for 18–20 minutes until the filling is just set but still slightly wobbly in the center.
6. Serve warm or cold, topped with a dollop of whipped cream and sprinkled with a little grated nutmeg.

2

3

4

## Pumpkin Pie Pumpkin vs. Jack-o'-lantern

Did you know a different type of pumpkin is used for pies than the ones we carve for Halloween?

Pie pumpkins are much smaller than carving pumpkins, usually weighing between 1 and 6 pounds. Their insides are also sweeter than carving pumpkins.

On the inside of carving pumpkins, you'll find softer and stringier flesh and lots of seeds to scoop out before you can do your carving.

# Sweet Potato Cupcakes with Coconut and Lime Frosting

**Makes:** 18
**Prep:** 20–25 mins
**Bake:** 1 hr

**Ingredients**

2 sweet potatoes
¾ cup all-purpose flour
2 teaspoons baking powder
½ teaspoon baking soda
½ teaspoon ground ginger
¼ teaspoon salt
⅔ cup granulated sugar
½ cup solid coconut oil
2 large eggs
toasted coconut flakes, to garnish
lime zest, to garnish

1. Preheat the oven to 425°F.
2. Place the sweet potatoes on a baking tray and bake for 45 minutes. Let cool, then peel. Puree in a food processor until smooth. Set aside.
3. Lower the oven temperature to 350°F. Line two 9-cup tins with paper liners.
4. Sift together the flour, baking powder, baking soda, ginger, and salt in a bowl.
5. Put the sugar and oil into a separate bowl, then beat with a hand mixer until light and fluffy. Beat in the eggs one at a time, alternating with the flour mixture. Stir in the sweet potato puree.
6. Spoon the mixture into each muffin liner, filling each about two-thirds full. Bake for 15–20 minutes, turning the tins halfway through the cooking time, until a fork or toothpick inserted into the center comes out clean. Leave to cool for 10 minutes, then transfer to a wire rack and leave to cool completely.
7. Spread the frosting on the cupcake tops. Garnish with toasted coconut flakes and lime zest.

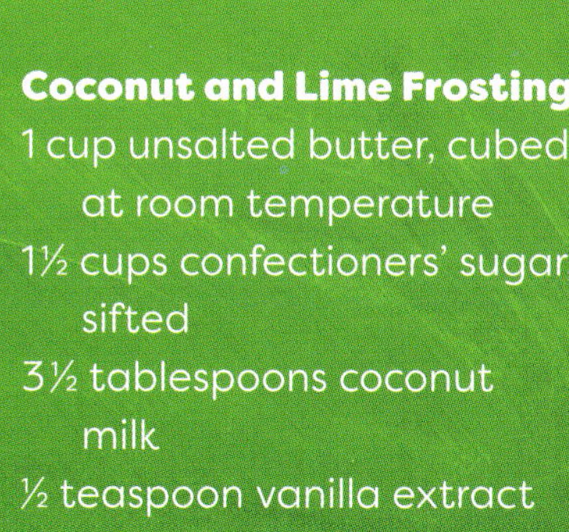

**Coconut and Lime Frosting**

- 1 cup unsalted butter, cubed, at room temperature
- 1½ cups confectioners' sugar, sifted
- 3½ tablespoons coconut milk
- ½ teaspoon vanilla extract
- ⅓ teaspoon salt
- ½ tablespoon **lime** zest
- 1 tablespoon lime juice

To make the frosting, put the butter and confectioners' sugar into a bowl, then blend in a food processor for 1 minute until fluffy. Beat in the remaining ingredients.

## How to Zest a Lime

1. Wash and dry the lime before zesting.
2. With a grown-up's help, hold a zester in one hand and the lime in the other.
3. Over a cutting board or bowl (to collect the zest as it falls), carefully push the lime away from you, across the rough side of the zester's blade.
4. Slowly rotate the lime as you zest. Be careful to not zest too much skin off because you'll remove the pith—the white part of a fruit's skin—which tastes very bitter.

# What Is Ginger?

Ginger is a root vegetable that's used as a spice. It can be used to make tea, can be pickled, or grated to use in recipes. People even make ginger candy!

Ginger has to be peeled before it can be cooked. You can use the side of a spoon to scrape off the top layer of skin. Now it can be chopped for cooking.

# Ginger & Chocolate Bars

**Makes:** 12
**Prep:** 10 mins
**Bake:** 15–20 mins, plus chilling

**Ingredients**

¾ cup unsalted butter, plus extra for greasing
½ cup brown sugar
3 tablespoons honey
2 pieces **ginger**, finely chopped
1½ cups oats

**Chocolate Glaze**

6 ounces chocolate, broken into pieces
3 tablespoons unsalted butter

1. Preheat the oven to 350°F. Grease a 9x13-inch shallow baking dish.
2. Put the butter, sugar, and honey into a large saucepan over low heat. Heat until melted. Remove from the heat and stir in the chopped ginger and oats.
3. Spoon the mixture into the prepared baking dish and smooth into an even layer. Bake for 15–20 minutes until pale golden. Leave to cool in the dish.
4. To make the glaze, put the chocolate and butter into a heatproof bowl over a saucepan with about 1 inch of gently simmering water. Heat until melted. Stir until smooth, then spread over the cooled bars. Chill in the refrigerator for 1 hour or until set. Cut into 12 bars.

# Beet Brownie Bites

**Makes** 36
**Prep:** 25 mins
**Bake:** 25–30 mins

**Ingredients**

oil, for greasing
⅔ cup semisweet chocolate, broken into small pieces
2 eggs
1 teaspoon vanilla extract
⅓ cup firmly packed brown sugar
⅓ cup oil
4½ cooked **beets**, mashed
¾ cup all-purpose flour
¾ teaspoon baking powder
3 tablespoons unsweetened cocoa powder

**1.** Preheat the oven to 350°F.

**2** Lightly grease an 8-inch square baking pan and line with parchment paper.

**3.** Place the chocolate in a heatproof bowl set over a saucepan of gently simmering water. Heat until chocolate is just melted. Remove from heat.

**4.** Put the eggs, vanilla extract, and sugar into a bowl. Mix using a hand mixer on high speed until pale and frothy. Beat in the oil, then stir in the beets.

5. Sift in the flour, baking powder, and cocoa, then fold in. Add the melted chocolate and stir evenly.
6. Spoon the batter into the prepared pan. Bake for 25–30 minutes until just firm to the touch. Let cool in the pan, then remove the parchment and place on a wire rack to cool completely.
7. Cut into about 36 bite-size squares to serve.

## Why Beets and Chocolate?

The combination of chocolate and beets may seem unusual, but it's actually a great pairing. Together, beets and chocolate deliver many vitamins, minerals, and antioxidants.

They also work well together in baked goods. Beets add an earthy taste when baked, like in a chocolate cake, and can help make cake moist and dense.

# Cooking Techniques & Methods

**BOIL**
to heat liquid, usually on a stove, until it reaches a high temperature and starts to bubble

**FRY**
to cook something in a type of fat (like butter or oil) over high heat, usually in a frying pan

**SAUTÉ**
to cook something quickly in a hot pan using a small amount of fat

**CHOP**
to cut food into small pieces

**DICE**
to cut food into cubes

**GRATE**
to make food smaller by scraping it on a rough surface

**MINCE**
to cut food finely, or very small pieces

**PEEL**
to remove the skin from a fruit or vegetable

**ZEST**
to remove the rind, or skin, of a citrus fruit

## BAKE

to cook something using dry heat, usually in an oven

## BROIL

to cook something by exposing it to extreme heat

## PREHEAT

to bring an oven to a specific temperature before baking

## BEAT

to mix by stirring quickly, usually in a circular motion

## DRIZZLE

to pour a liquid over food in a thin stream

## FOLD

to add a light ingredient to a heavier ingredient by gently mixing in a top to bottom motion

## GARNISH

food used to decorate a meal or plate

## GREASE

to rub a type of fat on a baking dish or cooking surface to prevent food from sticking to it

## PUREE

blending or mashing food together until it turns to a smooth consistency

## SIFT

to put a dry ingredient, like flour or baking soda, through a mesh strainer to add air to it and to get rid of any lumps

# Index